EDA: AN ANTHOLOGY OF
CONTEMPORARY TURKISH POETRY

What if you slept
And what if
In your sleep
You dreamed
And what if
in your dream
You went to heaven
And there plucked a strange and beautiful flower
And what if
When you awoke
You had that flower in your hand
Ah, what then?
                    —Samuel Taylor Coleridge, *Biographica Literaria*

Whenever I become the Sultan holding a lily
I'll give you a city of long syllables
As you enter it, its gates will disappear, empty.
                    —Ece Ayhan, *The Sultan With a Lily*

EDA: AN ANTHOLOGY OF CONTEMPORARY TURKISH POETRY

Edited, with an Introduction, by

Murat Nemet-Nejat

Preface by Talât Sait Halman

TALISMAN HOUSE, PUBLISHERS • JERSEY CITY, NEW JERSEY

Published in the United States of America by
Talisman House, Publishers
P.O. Box 3157
Jersey City, New Jersey 07303-3157

Manufactured in the United Sates of America
Printed on acid-free paper

ISBN: 1-58498-034-6

ACKNOWLEDGMENTS: We gratefully acknowledge the following for their support for this anthology and/or for granting us permission to include material for which they control the rights. We are grateful to the New York State Council for the Arts for their grant to support work on the anthology and to P.E.N. for sponsoring this grant. We are grateful to Esther Allen, the head of the P.E.N. Translation Committee, for spreading the news of the anthology and Lynda Morgan for helping in the grant application process. Unless otherwise indicated, works appear by permission of the authors, the translators, and/or their representatives. For their translations, prepared especially for this anthology, we are deeply grateful to Saliha Paker, Önder Otçu, Simon Pettet, Ülker İnce, Sidney Wade, Talât Sait Halman, Jordan Davis, Gary Sullivan, Maggie Dubris, Taner Bayers, Selhan Savcigil, Clifford Endres, and Mustafa Ziyalan. We are grateful to Enis Batur, without whose support this project could never have been completed, and to Nermin Mollaoğlu, who was there to help at all the right moments. Yapi Kredi Cultural Activities Arts and Publishing, Inc., gave permission for the translations of works by Faruk Nafiz Çamlıbel, Sait Faik, Ahmet Hamdi Tanpınar, Asaf Hâlet Çelebi, Celâl Sılay, Behçet Necatigil, İlhan Berk, Metin Eloğlu, Turgut Uyar, Cemal Süreya, Ece Ayhan, Gültan Akin, Ahmet Güntan, Lale Müldür, Seyhan Erözçelik, and Sami Baydar. We are grateful to the following for permission for translations: İstanbul Fetih Cemiyeti for Yahya Kemal Beyatlı, Gündüz Vassaf for Nâzım Hikmet, Filinta Önal for Ahmet Arif, Gendas Culture Publishing for küçük İskender, Büyük Doğu Yayinlari for Necip Fazil Kisakürek, Sami Rifat for Oktay Rifat, Mrs. Melih Cevdet Anday for Melih Cevdet Anday, Cahit Külebi's son and daughter for Cahit Külebi, Arif Damar for his own work, Özdemir İnce for his own work, Melisa Erdonmez Gürpınar for Melisa Gürpınar, Varlık Yayınları for Haydar Ergülen, Gülseli Inal for Nilgün Marmara, Mustafa Ziyalan for his own work, Didem Madak for her own work, and Metis Yayinları for the passages from Zeynep Sayın's İmgemın Pornografisi (2003). Translations by Murat Nemet-Nejat of "The Nigger in the Photograph," "Epitafio," and the three "Orthodoxies" by Ece Ayhan are reprinted from Ece Ayhan, The Black Cat Black and Orthodoxies, translated by Murat Nemet-Nejat (Los Angeles: Sun & Moon Press, 1997). Reprinted by permission of Sun & Moon Press. Translations by Murat Nemet-Nejat of Orhan Veli Kanik are reprinted from Orhan Veli Kanik, I, Orhan Veli, translated by Murat Nemet-Nejat (Brooklyn, NY: Hanging Loose Press, 1989). Reprinted by permission of the publisher. Most of the translations and essays were prepared especially for this volume. Particular attention has been given to identifying those who control copyright material reproduced here. Should any have been inadvertently missed, the error will be corrected, and proper acknowledgment given, in future printings.

To Karen, Danny and Rafi

and

To Louis Kahn's Bangladesh Parliament

CONTENTS

ESSAYS

PREFACE: *On EDA*

by Talât Sait Halman

"Bridge" stands paramount in Murat Nemet-Nejat's real and metaphorical world. Significantly, his first literary achievement was a book-length poem entitled *The Bridge*, an ambitious work that invited comparison with the vision and virtuosity of Hart Crane's masterpiece. Born of Iranian parents and raised in Istanbul, where he was educated at Robert College, the oldest American school outside the United States, his orientation has been rich in diverse cultures. Since his entry into the literary world in the 1960's, he has crossed and built many bridges linking disparate cultures, languages, and symbolic territories. No wonder his critical judgments in *Eda: An Anthology of Contemporary Turkish Poetry* bring to the fore Istanbul as the locus of Turkey's modern mythology and the quintessence of Turkish aesthetics. He grew up in Istanbul, the world's only metropolis that straddles two continents (Asia and Europe). The city also embraces the three Abrahamic religions, countless faiths and creeds, an infinite number of cultures and cults, ancient heritage and modernity. Conceivably, in his formative years, Murat Nemet-Nejat imagined bridges over the Bosporus like the two that Leonardo da Vinci had designed in the early sixteenth century. His poetic vision came to fruition in the 1970's and 1980's with the construction of two graceful bridges over the Bosporus. Murat Nemet-Nejat has devoted much of his literary life to transposing Turkish poetry into English. His is a bridge rare and daring.

Eda is itself a bridge that links Nemet-Nejat's three persona — poet, translator, critic. Although it identifies itself as an anthology, it is essentially an exploration into aspects of modern Turkish poetry, an effort to bring critical

1

appreciation to its terra incognita. Nemet-Nejat, who ranks as a principal translator of the beguiling modernist Orhan Veli Kanık (1914-1950) and the perplexing avant-gardist Ece Ayhan (1931-2002) expands his range here. His anthology encompasses antecedents of Turkey's poetic revolution, Ahmet Haşim (1887-1933) and Yahya Kemal Beyatlı (1884-1958), as well as such relative newcomers as Lale Müldür (1956-) and Didem Madak (1970-). Most of the leading figures are featured in *Eda* although surprisingly the great living master, Fazıl Hüsnü Dağlarca (1914-), and several other important innovators are missing. This anthology does not purport to be wholly representative. Rather, it prefers to make its points, in the poems it includes as well as in its critical evaluations, selectively and schematically. It is very much a poet's work, not a scholarly study. Its unorthodox, occasionally iconoclastic, ideas are bound to stimulate debate and controversy, especially among Turkey's conservative literary critics.

Murat Nemet-Nejat's critical style is refreshingly lyrical. His cultural and literary analyses are impressionistic, often rich in their images and sensuality. The poems and the critical assessment in *Eda*, in effect, replicate the synthesis of modern Turkish poetry.

As translator, Nemet-Nejat is inventive in all senses of the term. His insights into meaning, subtlety, metaphoric system, symbols, and rhythms not only empower but also slant his critical faculty. Often, he liberates the originals from their formal or conceptual stringencies — and sometimes seems to have written new poems in English out of the quintessences of his Turkish material. There are times when he takes only two lines of a much longer poem or when he reconstructs in an effort to reinterpret. For Nemet-Nejat, translation is an act of re-creation.

The concept of *eda* is focal, not a fanciful title. Originally a Persian noun, it was employed in Ottoman Turkish in the sense of "style" or "mannerism" or even "affectation." The eminent neo-classical poet Yahya Kemal Beyatlı (d. 1958) reintroduced it as a literary term signifying "distinctive poetic style." For

Nemet-Nejat, *eda* stands as the variegated essence of all the authentic hallmarks of Turkish culture and poetry. In an important sense, it is what makes Turkish poetic creativity both universal and uniquely original. Nemet-Nejat's *Eda* is a probing and provocative venture into that compelling terra firma.

THE IDEA OF A BOOK

As much as a collection of translations of poems and essays, this book is a translation of a language. Due to the fortuitous convergence of historical, linguistic and geographic factors, in the twentieth century — from the creation of the Turkish Republic in the 1920's to the 1990's when Istanbul/ Constantinople/Byzantium turned from a jewel-like city of contrasts of under a million into a city of twelve million — Turkey created a body of poetry unique in the twentieth century, with its own poetics, world view, and idiosyncratic sensibility. What is more, these qualities are intimately related to the nature of Turkish as a language — its strengths and its defining limits. As historical changes occurred, the language in this poetry responded to them, flowered, changed, but always remained a continuum, a psychic essence, a dialectic which is an arabesque. It is this silent melody of the mind — the cadence of its total allure — which this collection tries to translate. While every effort has been made to create the individual music of each poem and poet, none can really be understood without responding to the movement running through them, through Turkish in the twentieth century. I call this essence *eda*, each poet, poem being a specific case of *eda*, unique stations in the progress of the Turkish soul, language.

In *The Task of the Translator*, Walter Benjamin says that what gives a language *translatability* is its distance from the host language. *Eda* is this distance.

The otherness of *eda* has three aspects, thematic, linguistic, and meta-physical, together forming its core, essence:

4

a) Thematic: Istanbul, Mistress —Constantinople, Ward of The Virgin Mary

Istanbul, the city of unspeakable beauty; the city of stench, crooked streets, endless vice; the long coveted prize of the Islamic Ottoman Empire; the vulnerable, beloved, cherished spiritual center of Eastern Christianity; the site of the rational, tent-like simplicity of Turkish Imperial architecture;* the awesome interior space of Hagia Sofia; the European and Asian city; the city of crossings and bridges and double crosses; the city gorgeous to the eye, even more beautiful in its secrets; the city of spiritual yearning and impulse murder; the city of disco bars whose basement forms a Byzantine palace;† the city of violet water; the city of trysts; the city where place names gain fetishistic value; the city where life and history are cheap, and they are both everywhere.

The paradoxical nature of Istanbul is the obsessive reference point of twentieth-century Turkish poetry. Almost no poem is untouched by it — its shape, its street names, its people, objects and activities, its geographic and historical locus. As the city evolves, the poetry responds, trying to re-organize, make sense of the changes. This interplay between city and language resonates spiritually, erotically, politically, philosophically.

b) Linguistic: " am am a sea vermin, so human goose the block of ice on which i fly is *[souljam]*"

Turkish is an agglutinative language, that is to say, declensions occur inside the words as suffixes. Words need not be attached to either end of prepositions to spell out relationships, as in English. This quality gives Turkish total syntactical flexibility. Words in a sentence can be arranged in any permutable order, each sounding natural.

---

*In his *Journals*, Herman Melville sees in Ottoman mosques the simple design of a tent, the habitation form in Central Asian steppes from which the Ottoman Turks came.

†*The city of disco bars whose basement forms a Byzantine palace*: This is literally true in the Laleli district in Istanbul where the rooms of a Byzantine palace, with its columns intact, are used as basement storage space by businesses above.

The underlying syntactical principle is not logic, but emphasis: a movement of the speaker's or writer's affections. Thinking, speaking in Turkish is a peculiarly visceral activity, a record of thought emerging. The nearer the word is to the verb in a sentence, which itself has no fixed place in the sentence, the more emphasis it has. This ability to stress or unstress — not sounds or syllables; Turkish is syllabically unaccented — but words (thought as value-infested proximity) gives Turkish a unique capability for nuance, for a peculiar kind of intuitive thought.

Eda is the play of ideas through the body of Turkish. Not only is it the poetics of Turkish poetry in the twentieth century, it is the extension of the language itself, the flowering of its inherent potentials.

The otherness of *eda* is the distance which separates Turkish from English. English is an amazingly plastic language in terms of analytic thought, must spell out the relations between objects, between thoughts. A word like "from" or "to" predetermines the words which must precede and follow it. English permits a thought to be sayable only after being analyzed, socialized, objectified. This is the mystery of its rigid syntax after the Enlightenment. It resists, syntactically ostracizes — by being unnatural — pre-analytic thought, encouraging, recording the objective, tradition, socialized thought.

Eda is the alien other. What is this alien ghost, the way of moving and perceiving which must enter and possess English? It is Sufism, the Asiatic mode of perception which contains an intense subjectivity at its center. The pre-Islamic origins of Sufism are in Central Asian Shamanism. Turkish was the language of that area; its grammar is the quintessential Sufi language.

Before going any further, it should be said that Turkish has no gender distinctions, either he or she or it. Though one may assume that the specificity of the situation would make it clear, this is not quite so. In Sufism (and the poetry of *eda*) the distinction (any distinction) does not truly exist; *it* (a bird, for example) is a link between the divine (he/she/it) and human (he/she), with the constant possibility of movement among them. Pronouns are fungible, conceptionally their references unstable. Suppose an English sentence where

6

the pronoun (so gender and reference specific) shifts in the middle, lopsiding the syntactical balance.

(c) Metaphysical: Sufi Contradictions and *Arcs of Ascent and Descent*

In its pre-Islamic origins, Sufism unifies contradictions, more precisely, perceives, intuits experience before it splits into opposites. Islam introduces a mathematical language into this intuition. God, the lover, and the human lover are one, turning to and into each other, through a process both violent and loving.

Arcs of Descent and Ascent describe this process, movements from the unity of God to phenomenal multiplicity and the reverse, from multiplicity to unity. These movements are simultaneous, not sequential — two aspects of one divine essence. The supreme moment in Sufism is the sudden shift in perception when a *state* (in its multiple senses) of exile, of accelerating multiplicity and distance, is experienced as yearning, a re-unifying movement, yearning, towards home, God. The shift is in perception, that is, in the mind. Everything, every object in existence, particularly physical love, move towards this moment. That is the radical subjectivity — love as objective subjectivity — at the heart of Sufism.

Sufism embodied in *eda* is different from Mevlana Jalaloddin Rumi's, with which the West is more familiar. Rumi's supreme process is ecstasy, reached through wine and dancing. On a linguistic level God and the speaker remain distinct, "You" and "I." Sufi union with God is expressed philosophically, metaphorically, harmonically.

In the Turkish tradition the supreme Sufi act is weeping, the dissolution of the individual ego by suffering through love, loss, the liquid of tears. What is ecstatic in *eda* involves a blurring of identities, in pain, at the same time, moving from object to object, unifying them in a mental movement of yearning, dance of dispossession. Wine has to be bought; tears are for free. No

7

gendered pronouns, no stable word order, Turkish is a tongue of radical melancholia.

Distinctions dissolve into union. Here is the paradox of simultaneity in the *arcs of descent and ascent*. A waking state enters another's dream, and vice versa, creating a continuum. The objective becomes subjective. Physical desire ends in spiritual satiation. Weakness is also an expression of power. Pain is also pleasure. The Istanbul harbor with its crossing boats is a site of extreme beauty, paradise, and Styx, a separator and joiner of Europe and Asia, etc. The central sphere in *eda* is the moon, the prevailing light, moonlight: visible dark.

In its essence, this poetry has no metaphors (but creates spiritual stations of which Istanbul is the center) because no distinctions. Every image is a station, a physical sight in a spiritual progress of reincarnations, of yearning. Images and thoughts collapse towards each other, in love: "The rough man entered the lover's garden/It is woods now, my beautiful one, it is woods," says the sixteenth-century poet Pir Sultan Abdal.* *What* is the garden? The lover's pubic hair or a divine garden, *it*? *Who* is the "rough man"? The speaker, the speaker's lover or a third? *To* whom, by whom are the words uttered? In Turkish Sufism, consciousness (love) is not a matter of "You" and "I," but a triangle: you, I and he/she/It.

Here lies perhaps the crucial role of Istanbul in *eda*. Located on two continents, precious both to Christianity and Islam, with its endlessly contra-dictory nature, Istanbul becomes a site for a series of superimpositions.

In the essay "What children Say," Gilles Deleuze states:

> . . . a milieu is made up of qualities, substances, powers, and events: the street, for example, with its material (paving stones), its noises (the cries of merchants), its animals (harnessed horses) or its dramas (a horse slips, a horse falls down, a horse is beaten. . .). The trajectory merges not only with the subjectivity of those who travel through a

---

*Pir Sultan Abdal's poem is quoted in full in *A Godless Sufism: Ideas on Twentieth-Century Turkish Poetry* in the text section of the anthology.

milieu, but also *with the subjectivity of the milieu itself* [italics my own], insofar as it is reflected in those who travel through it.*

Istanbul is that milieu. *Eda* is the trajectory, poetics of a trip on a map. Sufism is its fusion of objectivity and subjectivity, a convergence of psychic time with history — the history of a city in twentieth century and of the soul of the folks passing through it.

History and Poetry:

I, in my room overlooking the seashore,
Not looking out of the window,
Know that the boats sailing out in the sea
Go loaded with watermelons.
—Orhan Veli

The first work in this anthology was first published in 1921, the last in 1997. During this period Turkish poetry underwent three major transformations. The first occurred between 1921, the publication of Ahmet Haşim's poem "That Space" ("O Belde") in his book *Lake Hours* (*Göl Saatleri*) and 1950, the year Orhan Veli died. During this period, for the first time in almost four hundred years, since the Azeri Turkish poet Fuzulî's *Leila and Majnun*, agglutidunal Turkish became a written literary language. There are four central poets in this period, Ahmet Haşim, Yahya Kemal Beyatlı, Nâzım Hikmet and Orhan Veli. Seemingly very different from each other, they all wrote in spoken Turkish, and, together, they established the backbone of *eda* in Turkish poetry.

Haşim and Beyatlı appear closer to the earlier Ottoman poetry in their sound (occasional use of the *gazel* form and rhymes) and vocabulary (use of

---

*Gilles Deleuze, *Essays: Critical and Clinical*, trans. Daniel W. Smith and Michael A. Greco (Minneapolis: U of Minnesota P, 1997), p. 61.

9

Persian and Arabic words). But the cadence of their language is Turkish, and each brings something new and essential to the language.

Haşim brings the shy, slightly feminine, sinuous, melancholy, linguistically self-conscious movement to Turkish poetry. The inherent potential in *eda* for yearning, long sentences, in the flight to make thought connections which sometimes tease with falling apart, originates with him.

Beyatlı's poetry sounds even closer to Ottoman poetry. The conventional view of him is that he is a formalist recreating in modern Turkish the classical sound of Ottoman forms — a poetry of Ottoman music. I think the view misses its importance. A philosophical pursuit runs through Beyatlı's formal sound and rhyme patterns. It is to transform conceptual splits of time (between past and present) and consciousness (between waking and sleeping states) into a continuum. This conceptual shift, the impulse to cross over, absent in Ottoman poetry, is an integral part of *eda*.

The pursuit undercuts, disrupts Beyatlı's poetry of "pure music" because the Ottoman *gazel*, of rhymed distinct units, does not contain Beyatlı's anti-formal sense of reality. Consequently, in my view, there is an an instability pushing against, potentially breaking through and toppling, discrete rhymed couplets. Sidney Wade's exquisite "Night" in the anthology translates Beyatlı's "pure music" as well as one can. "That Summer" and "Reunion" try to touch the inherent instability of thought pushing through the sound structure.

Nâzım Hikmet wrote his major poetry in the 1930's and 1940's while he was in jail not very far from Istanbul for Communist subversion. The poem/letters to his wife from jail are full of yearning for his wife, for Istanbul, for a better future for mankind, reminiscent of *eda*. Hikmet also started writing *Human Landscapes From My Country* (*Memleketimden İnsan Manzaraları*), possibly his central work, in the 1930's in jail. This is an epic the poet Ece Ayhan calls a *cinematic work*, which starts with the Turkish War of Independence and covers a range of Anatolian characters. In this poem Hikmet uses the Anatolian landscape as a space of psychic movement (at moments, language as a river) very much the way Istanbul is used in *eda*.

Starting with *835 Lines* (*835 Satır*) in 1929, any Ottoman echo in Hikmet's poetry disappears. Hikmet replaces old structures with two things: the rhythms, cadences of Anatolian folk poetry and the Russian poet Mayakovski's darting, staggered, futurist lines. These two elements remain constants — partly visual constants — in Hikmet's poetry. The darting line fragments often gain a sinuous melancholy, peculiarly Turkish.

Orhan Veli, who wrote his poetry also in the late 1930's and 1940's, represents the culmination of the first stage of *eda*. As an agglitudinal language the center of gravity of Turkish is not in words, but the cadences among them; the aura that movement creates. In his introduction to the manifesto/poetry-book *Strange* (*Garip*), Veli says, in Talât Sait Halman's translation: "I wish it were possible to dump language itself." Veli writes a minimalist poetry stripped of metaphors; what remains is pure cadence, its space. Poems which seem to be made of absolute inessentials are absolutely unforgettable. In him the link between *eda* and the rhythms of conversational Turkish becomes absolute.

Veli is the lightning rod of Turkish poetry. Every ensuing movement starts with an attack on him. For instance, Cemal Süreya partly starts the *Second New* movement (the first being Veli's and his friends' *Strange*) in an essay entitled "Orhan Veli's Mistake," attacking Veli's "limitations," for a poetry penetrating secrets. Here is what he says about Veli: "No line, no meter, no music, no image, no beauty, no rhymes, no metaphysics, no drama." Ironically, towards the end of his life, Süreya wrote powerful poems very reminiscent of Veli. Another *Second New* poet, Ece Ayhan, calls Veli a "watercolor poet"; but towards the end of the essay he mentions Veli's "portability," calling the poems folk songs. Another group calls Veli a "state" poet, suggesting that the popularity of Veli was pushed by the government to deflect attention from Hikmet's communist poetry. Veli keeps being read and re-read.

Before going on any further, one needs to mention a group of poems whose significance is often overlooked. From the 1930's into the 1950's some poets wrote in syllabic meters, often rhymed and derived from folk poetry. This work constitutes a distinct genre which I call *arabesque*. Arabesque has two meanings. First, it is the name of a popular musical genre started in the 1960's, becoming prevalent in the 1970's and 1980's, when a huge influx of Anatolian population turned Istanbul from one and a half million into a metropolis of twelve million. Arabesque is the music of truck, bus and taxi drivers, of waiters, of laborers, of street venders, etc., most of them Anatolian Muslims.

Arabesque poems project a religious consciousness which, nevertheless, embraces love as a profane, obsessive, rebellious act. Faruk Nafız Çamlıbel's "The Escaper" and Bedri Rahmi Eyuboğlu's "Black Mulberry" are examples of it.* The poems often have a street feel to them, similar to the American blues. Arabesque is the genre through which the Anatolian consciousness, its urban alienation, integrates itself into *eda*. In Cahit Külebi's poems, for example, the speaker is an Anatolian peasant talking to another Anatolian (often, a lover), Istanbul implicitly there, indirectly referred to as an alien third.

Most arabesque poems were written by the 1950's, before the arabesque had emerged as a musical genre. This is startling because Istanbul was still a discreet, relatively small city. The poems prophetically anticipate the Anatolian flux into the city — pre-writing its consciousness — and sing of a future to come. This premonitive response is the critical importance of the genre, sustaining *eda*'s intimate contact with the Turkish population.

The second meaning of arabesque is the elaborate, abstract decoration often inside mosques. An admirer of Beyatlı, Ahmet Hamdi Tanpınar writes arabesques in that sense, exquisitely modulated poems of "pure" Sufi music.

Perhaps, the most important arabesque poet is Necip Fazıl Kısakürek. Using both syllabic folk and Ottoman *gazel* forms, his poetry is obsessive, profane and religious, a poetry of the Sufi *arc of descent*. The *Second New* poet Ece Ayhan considers his poetry clunky, full of "high school" emotions. I think the baroque "clunkiness" is part of its arabesque identity, integral to its unforgettable power. Kısakürek's pursuit of lower depths, towards a remote

---

*Unfortunately, permission to reprint this poem was not obtained from Eyuboğlu's estate.

illumination, makes him one of the precursors of a 1990's poem like küçük İskender's *souljam* (*cangüncem*).

ᘛ ᘛ

She didn't fetch her hair along,
Kept it on the dresser, full of despair;
But her hair fell through the unlit cracks,
I undid her drawers
I drowned myself in her hair.
—Cemal Süreya

The *Second New* represents the second stage in *eda*. Officially, it starts in the 1960's with the magazine *Papyrus* (*Papirus*), edited by Cemal Süreya, in which he published new poets, including their critical essays. But the poems which start the *Second New*, the ones inside Cemal Süreya's first book *Pigeon English* (*Üvercinka*) and Ece Ayhan's *Miss Kınar's Waters* (*Kınar Hanımın Denizleri*) were written in the 1950's, by two young men in their twenties.

Though others belong to it it, the central poets of the *Second New* are Cemal Süreya, Ece Ayhan, and İlhan Berk. Their influence is sequential and forms stages in the development of *eda*, paralleling changes in the perceptions of Istanbul as a city.

The overweening thrust of the *Second New* is expanding consciousness, in depth (revealing secrets) and range of emotions (expanding poetic styles). That's why the *Second New* starts with a misreading (deliberate or not, maybe necessary) of Orhan Veli. *Pigeon English*, Süreya's first book, is a series of lyrics of seduction from the male point of view. What is amazing about them is the power dimension of the eroticism — love as a stripping of both the body and mystery. In spectacular image combinations, the poems implicate, seduce the reader into the act — keeping him or her grasping/gasping for objectivity. These image combinations are the great contribution of Süreya to Turkish

13

poetry. They release the sado-masochistic, subversive side of Sufism into contemporary Turkish.

A story underlies *Üvercinka*. In its middle, a woman rejects the speaker. By this, the power angle of the poems reverses to one of grief. Though never completely suppressing the other side, this changed point of view predominates in Süreya's later poetry. "In Your Country," for example, is a poem of dissolution through loss. In that respect, Süreya's development is within the central Sufi narrative of Fuzulî's *Leila and Majnun*, physical love changing into spiritual love. At the end of his life Süreya wrote beautiful, simple poems, the last one of which is, "After 12 P.M./All drinks/Are wine," lines of total acceptance, referring back to Ahmet Haşim and his predecessor Hafız. The beauty of these poems is reminiscent of Orhan Veli. Süreya comes full circle back to the Turkish poet he starts his poetic movement by attacking.

Ece Ayhan had to self-publish his first book, *Miss Kınar's Waters*. Instead of, like Süreya's exuding a seductive masculine eroticism, Ayhan's book is opaque, personal, trying to hide, as much as to reveal. *Miss Kınar's Waters* also has a story buried in it, that of a sister's suicide (possibly, from being seduced) and the grief surrounding such an event. All the poems are from the point of view of the victim, the weak, the powerless, including seduced children turned hustlers; many are gay. Even when the poem is from the angle of the seducer, e.g. in "Wall Street" ("Kambiyo"), the tone is elegiac. Eroticism is tinged with suppressed rage, which in flashes pierces through as implicit commentary. These flashes weave a melody whose emotional tone is lucid, transparent; but whose meaning eludes us, is veiled.

Miss Kınar's Waters and Ece Ayhan's ensuing two works, *A Blind Cat Black* (*Bakışsız Bir Kedi Kara*) and *Orthodoxies* (*Ortodoksluklar*), open up the suppressed, unofficial — but inescapably there — strata of the Turkish culture: the gay, the sexual criminals of all sorts, the ethnic minority Armenians, Greeks, and Jews, their slang and linguistic codes. His work is full of the burden of this revelation, simultaneously hiding and revealing, a revelation in the process of occurring.

In the poetry of the *Second New*, from the mid-1950's to the mid-1970's, Istanbul as a psychic landscape is sliced into four. The Bosporus divides the Asian from the European side and opens to the Istanbul harbor. Except for İlhan Berk, most of the poetry up to Ayhan, including Veli's and Süreya's, is focused on the Bosporus landscape. This is the Islamic, official side of Istanbul, a city of extreme beauty. Its eroticism, except for the short story writer Sait Faik whose casual, lackadaisical seeming style is saturated with an unpronounceable language, is heterosexual.

The second division occurs between the old city — the site of the Topkakı Palace, the major mosques and the Hagia Sophia, that is to say, the site of the old Byzantium which the Ottomans conquered — and the new city. The two parts are split by the Golden Horn, which is an extension of the Istanbul harbor. The Golden Horn creates a skyline of mosques on the old city side and is crossed by the Galata Bridge at the entrance to the harbor. The new city, built on a hill, is called Galata (or Pera). It is a district of crooked, winding streets where the Turkish minorities, Armenians, Greeks and Jews, reside; it also contains the red-light areas, divey bars, whore houses, transvestite corners of Istanbul.

Ece Ayhan brings Galata as the place of the forbidden, politically invisible, feminine into Turkish poetry; he expands Istanbul as a poetic landscape. He does it first through puns between the straight and street meanings of words. For instance, *Orthodoxies*, one of the titles of his books, refers to Orthodox Christianity and metaphorically to holiness, saintliness; but in slang the word means whoredom, homosexuality, pederasty, betrayal. His poetry is also permeated with people's or place names, often suggesting a secret, double life: Hamparsum, the famous Armenian composer of Ottoman music; Bald Hassan, a theatrical stock character always appearing with a broom; Peruz, a famous transvestite singer; Al-Qazar, at the time a theatre of adventure movies frequented by child molesters; Three Angels, a Christian chapel. Fetishistically, names are secret places in the body of Istanbul.

In the *Second New*, Istanbul has a distinct shape, that of a city of one and a half million split into the dichotomy of open and secret, old and new, Moslem and Levantine, straight and gay. The movement articulates its poetic project of expanding consciousness by working through the city in depth: Süreya by connecting the erotic (the secret) with power; seductions occur on the water, by a wall, etc.; Ayhan by mentioning names, expressions belonging to the social and historical underbelly of the city. This pursuit of secrets is the metaphysical resonance driving the *Second New* poets.

The association of Istanbul with feminine sensuality and a site/sight of secrets has been there since Byzantine times. When Herman Melville visited "Constantinople" almost exactly one hundred years before the *Second New*, he saw, reacted to the city exactly the same way: "The fog only lifted from about the skirts of the city, which [was] built upon a promontory. . . . It was a coy disclosure, a kind of coquetting, leaving room for the imagination & heightening the scene. Constantinople, like her Sultanas, was thus veiled in her 'ashmak'."* The bridge Melville crosses and re-crosses and writes about, the steep road where he feels lost in a crowd of people are more or less the same city, of about the same size, Süreya, Ayhan, and Turgut Uyar write about.

ও ও

like a bridge, departing from myself
like a Turk, red, I am crying *turkish red*
—Lale Müldür

The 1990's, the Poetry of Motion:

In broad outlines, the development of Turkish poetry in the twentieth century has a dialectic shape; major works got written almost simultaneously

---

*Herman Melville, *Journals* (Evanston and Chicago: Northwestern UP and the Newberry Library, 1989), p. 58.

16

by Haşim and Beyatlı, Hikmet and Veli, Süreya and Ayhan, interspersed with relatively fallow stretches. The years between the middle of the 1970's to the late 1980's was such a fallow period.

From the onset of the *Second New*, a crucial event undermining the movement started to occur; Istanbul began its exponential growth. The first shot of this process was a twentieth-century Haussmann project in the late 1950's. The Menderes government tore down the historical district of Aksaray to build a multi-laned road to accommodate the upcoming flood of Anatolian population into the city. By the early 1980's two bridges had been built over the Bosporus (one of the psychic dividers of Istanbul's landscape) and many of the beautiful old *konaks* (villas) on it (areas Beyatlı, Veli, Uyar wrote about) were destroyed. Istanbul had been transformed from a city of secrets and depth into a nexus of movement, a sprawling, global metropolis.

Here lies the poetic crisis of the 1970's and 1980's. Poets struggling with the legacy of the *Second New* faced a city which corresponded less and less to it. How to find a poetic language reflecting the new shape of the city, making it once more part of a spiritual language?

The poetry of this transformed landscape exploded, once again, almost simultaneously in a series of poems and books published between 1991 and 1997: Lale Müldür's "Waking to Constantinople" ("Konstantinopolis'e Uyanmak") in *A Book of Series (Seriler Kitabı)*, Sami Baydar's lyric poems the first book of which is *The Gentlemen of the World (Dünya Efendileri, 1987)*, Ahmet Güntan's *Romeo and Romeo (Romeo ve Romeo)*, küçük İskender's *souljam (cangüncem)*, Seyhan Erözçelik's "Coffee Grinds" in *Rose and Coffee Grinds (Gülve Telve)* and Enis Batur's *East-West Dîvan (Doğu-Bati Dîvanı)*.

These works share crucial similarities. First, they are all essentially poems of movement, rather than depth. In *Romeo and Romeo* two lovers move around each other in an abstract dance to reach an elusive center. The most striking aspect of *souljam* is the chaotic, expansive energy which spins fragments, seemingly at random, away from each other, though a cadence of yearning runs through and unifies them. "Coffee Grinds" is twenty-four Rorschach tests made of coffee grinds over which the eye spins meandering narratives of fortune and hope, cajoled by a listener. In the narratives in *East-West Dîvan*, the teller and listener are fused in a continuous weaving motion. In Sami Baydar's poems, images, like water, keep changing without any definable logic, tracing the sinuous contour of something invisible; waves point to the space between them ("The Sea Bird"), a pitcher to the water inside ("Pitcher"), biographical fragments to the soul running through the fragments ("Jacket").

In the poetry of the 1990's Istanbul changes from a physical place into an idea, an elusive there, a basically mystical, dream space of pure motion. In no poem is this clearer than in Müldür's "Waking to Constantinople." In it the contemporary urban sprawl of Istanbul is reimagined as a historical sprawl during which the city was continuously destroyed and rebuilt. In Möbius-like connections, the poem weaves a synthesis between the Byzantine dream world and Ottoman rationality, time opening up as a continuum, and Istanbul dialectically being given a new name.

"Waking to Constantinople" achieves its conceptual links through long, sinuous lines which almost become prose. The teasing with the limits of a poetic line is a stylistic identifying mark of four of the poems mentioned above. Through it often depth turns into a poetry of motion. The long poetic line was created by İlhan Berk, the third poet associated with the *Second New*. His work makes the explosion of the 1990's possible; in him one sees how movements of the mind and Istanbul as the city of motion join.

*

THE GARDEN DETESTS CALENDESTINE OPERATIONS
—İlhan Berk

Though associated with the *Second New*, Berk's poetry has little to do with depth, everything to do with motion. Born before Süreya and Ayhan and still alive — that is to say, writing more than sixty years — his work assimilates the poetic movements from Hikmet and Veli on. The great pleasure of Berk's poetry is to follow his agile mind weaving in and out of historical time periods, following the contours of crooked streets in Galata, naming names, or stopping at a now defunct whore house listening to the voices of women there. In "Garlic," ostensibly a prose piece, time as a layered entity with past and present disappears and becomes a unified place of the spirit, of mind play.

In Berk, Süreya's sense of unexpected connections and Ayhan's awareness that Istanbul is a mongrel accumulation floating on a sea of history are unified into a flat tapestry of pure motion, an irreligious but still spiritual space where splits associated with time are abandoned. Berk's poetry reveals no secrets but lights everything it touches with its inflections.

From the 1950's on, everything Berk wrote is associated with his "long poetic line." To understand what that line is, one can go to a Haşim poem, the first poet in the anthology: "In a grieving perfection's insomnia. . . ." Why is perfection associated with insomnia? Insomnia is the most intense state of wakefulness (consciousness) because it is nearest sleep. This is a poetics of limits, a motion of the mind towards zero, the unreachable, the forbidden.

Berk's long poetic line approaches the limit of prose, growing in intensity doing so. A lot of Berk's best poems look like prose; they are continuous strips of poetic line moving towards and away from a limit. Here lies the essential paradox of Berk and Turkish poetry. He seems to be the most pagan, least religious of poets, as Turkish poetry rarely is about religion. But an irreducible spiritual essence runs through both of them, as it does in Veli or Haşim or Hikmet or Süreya or İskender or Güntan. . . . It is buried in the agglutinative cadences of Turkish, a language of affections inflected by proximity to a movable, elusive verb — a dance towards and away from limits. The sensual, metaphysical and historical are unified in this movement — the *eda* — a continuum of earth, water and human habitation:

19

. . .

I SEE THE HOUSE AFTER I LEAVE THE GARDEN BEHIND.

To compare the garden and the house: the garden is wide open in the face of the close-mouthed, conservative quality the house characterizes (permeated with that despotism which wounded it long ago).

THE GARDEN DETESTS CALENDESTINE OPERATIONS.

Full of sound and voices.
Its face overflowing into the street.
Offering a female reading.

To compare them, it is sexual (what is not?)

THE HOUSE IS MORE AS IF TO DIE IN THAN TO LIVE IN.

Oh garden, the muddy singer of the street.

"Dirty Child."

Hello gardens, here I am!

—İlhan Berk, from "Houses,"
translated by Önder Otçu

ฺ   ฺ

Unless otherwise specified, the translations in this anthology are my own. They run the gamut from being absolutely literal to a few where I took liberties.

But in all I tried to be absolutely faithful to what I believe their essences are. My attempt was always to translate that essence without diluting it. I followed the same principle choosing the translations of others.

Any failures in this intention belong to me.

There are two poems the omissions from this anthology I regret deeply. One is Bedri Rahmi Eyuboğlu's "Black Mulberry" ("Karadut") and the other Can Yücel's "A Parable" ("Mesel"), but I could not obtain permission from the poet's estates to do so. "Black Mulberry" is an exquisite example of the arabesque poem. "A Parable " is one of the sharpest and wittiest political poems of the 1970's.

I have tried to date the poems whenever possible. This is important because the growth of Turkish poetry has an inner logic. Also, a few major poets before the 1960's, particularly Beyatlı and Hikmet, did not have their works published in book form until decades later than when they wrote them. One of the wonders of Turkish poetry is that the influence of these poets often does not start with their publications, but with their writing. The succeeding poets seems to integrate their achievements as if through osmosis, in response to a wider linguistic and cultural process to which they belong.

Whenever there was an option, I chose the earliest available date, either the date of the writing given by the poet or the publication date in a magazine or in the book in which the poem appears.

∽ ∽

I would like to thank Ed Foster of Talisman Publishers for his endless patience giving me enough time and space to make this anthology the best I could.

I would like to thank the poet and director of Yapi Kredi Yayinlari Mr. Enis Batur and his assistant Ms. Nermin Mollaoglu for their generous and invaluable help in securing the permissions to publish the translations of many poets in this anthology. I would also like to thank Professor Talât Sait Halman and Professor Suat Karantay for their intimate knowledge of Turkish literary culture which helped me trace the copyright ownership of a few poets whose estates would have been impossible to trace otherwise. I would like to thank Professor Saliha Paker for her enthusiasm for the book and her spreading its news in Turkey.

I would like to thank my poet friend Mustafa Ziyalan for his invaluable effect on the anthology. The idea of *eda* which is essential to this book was first mentioned by him though I may have carried the concept into directions with which he may not agree. I would like to thank Simon Pettet for reading many translations in their early versions and who first sensed the "Turkish music" as the translations evolved.

I would to thank my wife Karen Nemet-Nejat for her patience and understanding the endless hours I had to shut myself up in a room. I would like to thank my two children, Daniel and Rafael, for being in my life.

Finally, I would like to thank my business, Murat Oriental Rugs, Inc., for the financial sacrifices it had to make for the writing of this book.

POETRY

AHMET HAŞİM (1885-1933)

THAT SPACE

Out of the sea
this thin air blowing, let it play with your hair
if you knew
one who, with the pain of yearning, looked at the setting east,
you too, with those eyes, that sadness are beautiful!
Neither you
nor I
nor that evening gathered around your beauty
nor that harbor from the sea,
for painful thoughts,
knows closely the generation unfamiliar
with melancholy.
The present
who calls you only a thin young lady
who calls me only a fool,
the calamitous appetite, this dirty
stare,
can't find in you or me
a meaning,
or in this evening a delicate
anxiety
or in the placid sea
a resentment,
a tremor of turning inward and wanting nothing.

You and I
and the sea
and this evening without tremors, silent.
sifting up as if your soul's odor,
far
and freed from a land full of blue shadows
and in this parted space of exile forever
sentenced.

That space?
Remains in the virginal, vertiginous territories of dreaming,
a blue evening
constantly resting in it.
the sea on your skirt
pitches into the soul the quiet
of sleep.
Women there are thin, pure and nocturnal,
in their eyes your melancholy,
either they are sisters or lovers,
wise to the ways of assuaging the heart
pain
or your tearful lips
or or the purple quiet of questions in your eyes,
Their souls are the condensed
violet of resentful evenings
constantly looking for
quietus.
The unlit fire of the moon's sadness,
as if, only hidden in your hands,
they are so awkward, ah, those hands,
their dumb and partaken melancholy

and the preoccupied evening, that sick water
they all resemble each other there . . .

That space,
in what continent of dreams,
snaked by what what river?
Is it a lying place or true,
but an undiscoverable shelter of dreams?
Don't know . . . I only know
you and I
and the blue sea
and this evening which stirs in me
the strings of melancholy and
inspiration,
far
and freed from a land full of blue shadows
and in this parted space of exile forever
sentenced.

1921

GLASS

Don't think it's rose, or tulip,
filled with fire, don't hold it, you burn,
this rosy glass.

Fuzulî had drunk of this fire*
Majnun, fallen with its elixir
into the state of this poem.

Those drinking from this cup burning
why, filling the night of love
with moans and mint, end to end

Filled with fire, don't hold it you burn
this rosy glass.

1921

Fuzulî: The sixteenth-century Azeri Turkish poet who wrote *Leila and Majnun*. Majnun falls in love with Leila and, being refused, goes mad, begins wandering on the countryside, talks to animals, becomes a poet. His love becomes transformed to spiritual love. This is the central story of Turkish Sufism.

In a grieving perfection's insomnia
Why your insistence, nightingale?
Listen, in the orchards of our heart
The rose you mentioned gave its life.

Spreading, the rose now in the air
In a new abundance.

1921

ASCENSION

you'll ascend the stairs slowly
on your skirts a golden pile of leaves
always you'll be looking at the East crying

Always looking at the East crying to be revived

waters are yellowing . . . your face paling in shadows
bending roses bleed bleeding to the ground
wait flame like on branches nightingale
has water burnt why is the marble bronze

*From yellow to bronze to crimson to night is the fiery movement of
the soul in its ascent.*

*Fire is reflected light in the evening twilight, soon to be replaced by
the reflected light of the moon.*

*The nightingale and the branch on which it stands become one,
waiting together.*

wait flame like on branches nightingale

look at the crimson sky turning evening

1926

Out of the beloved's lip
a carat of fire is this carnation
my soul knows it, its pain.

As it falls, it's hit around.
butterflies reeking of anger
my soul wheeling round . . .

1923

A river of fire
between your soul and mine
mine unburdened itself
of this love's impossible wound

As this glitter reflected on her
I ran away from that look, that lip
I looked at her silently, from far,
as this river reflected on her . . .

1921

YAHYA KEMAL BEYATLI
(1884-1958)

THAT SUMMER

Was a summer reverie, summer, written by your desire
Each second, color, poem of satiation,
The garden still plethora, with your sweetest voice
If one day you long back oh for a station of that summer

Look at the nodding water of the harbor, you'll see,*
That past night lying in its depth
The moon, large roses oh your most beautiful reflection,
In short, that summer reverie standing in its place.

---

*The harbor is the Istanbul harbor joining the Bosporus to the Sea of Marmara.

NIGHT
translated by Sidney Wade

While Kandilli* floated in clouds of sleep,
We pulled the full moon through the unruffled deep.

The path through the water was a shimmering burn.
We went . . . and never spoke of the return.

Dreaming slopes and phantom trees . . .
Hillsides in water taking their ease.

The season's nearing end was strewn
With the notes of an old and distant tune.

We lost ourselves in that long, far drift
Until it put us ashore in the dawn, and left.

---

*a village on the Bosporus

REUNION

"If the world becomes a dream, the dream in its turn becomes a world."

—Novalis

Those sleeping asleep with their beloved
feeling their reconstitution, in love
thinking time is a night of unending delight, unseeing
the lit horizon in the East
dreaming their dream is, eternal garden to
love, every season
summer, of a different
wind.
Of nightingale one hears no mourning scream
in that delight,
the rose or crescent moon not fade, nor
diminution, a sky dome every moment only blue, blue
to every eye,
the richest parallel
to poor,
love-pool dream in the wind,
as if endless, the far melody of the
spout.

A spirit in that deep garden if it lived once,
once her arms O'ing round its neck, O on its
laps, oblivious delirious, with her scent
in the air, the witchery
of love in every breath,
as if stars born from end to end, exiting
miraculous in the
eye,

unfooled, by the most ling'ring kiss, kissing
thirstier,
salt hungrier, secret
muddier, become
God.

They who are in that garden tinder with roses,
arriving by which coincidence
to me?
Love coaxing them fortune's
compassionate wind, light
in it,
this light of night, not
a chariot
in galloping race,
two souls unseeing the coming dawn seeing
a wider horizon
shining in their glance enflaming the sky
of torches.

Those sleeping asleep with their beloved
enduring all delight in that, satiation
the world forgotten in those waters
while heartless time-piece rings in, neglected time —
if at that moment the soul shakes from its blissful sleep
wakes to, dungeon firmament,
a catastrophic wakening
burning each day stunned with longing

oh servant, this darkness worse than Styx
oh sidekick, your heart belongs to Them
oh reunion, submit those lovers to your weavery,
oh, sweet and celestial night! Be endless!

FARUK NAFİZ ÇAMLIBEL
(1898-1973)

THE ESCAPER

They called you ugly, I became enemy to beauty;
They called you infidel, I gave up God;
You picked up gold coins tossed to you by countless hands,
Became a whore; I resented purity.

I didn't call you ugly, didn't call you infidel,
To me your curses were as holy as your religion,
You lived in my heart for five years, I didn't call you a guest,
When how did this escape occur to you?

My heart, caught in the steely strings of your beauty,
Will be dragged after you for centuries;
Even if like a doe you escape from mountain to mountain
My love will follow you like a pack of hounds . . .

1925

AHMET HAMDİ TANPINAR
(1901-1962)

WHOLE SUMMER

How well the whole summer passed,
nights in the small garden . . .
you white as lilies
and in a furtive thought . . .
as if in the full moon night
the reverie can't be crossed
becoming a palace
as if in house arrest
How well the whole summer passed,
nights in the small garden . . .

BAR

A Rose
offers itself
a coral wine glass
in
the bars
of time

. . .

ROADS TOO EARLY

Roads disappeared early
I lost my hope of disappearing
Something else covered your foot steps
Beyond the silence colored moon

Far away from everything, and stars
You became the denier of all gardens
Built your house where my freezing winds
Can't find a branch to break

NÂZIM HİKMET (1902-1963)

THE BLUE-EYED GIANT

He was a blue-eyed giant
He loved a tiny little woman
Her dream was a tiny little house
        with honey-suckles
            dappled
                in the garden.

The giant's love was like a giant's
And his hands were so built for big things
He could not build the frame
        ring the bell
        of the house
          with honey-suckles
        in the garden.

He was a blue-eyed giant
He loved a tiny little woman
Such tiny tiny woman
Felt famished for comfort
        tiring on the giant's road
And saying bye-bye to the blue-eyed giant
Entered on the arms of a rich midget
        the house

        with honey-suckles
        in the garden.

Now the blue-eyed giant understands
It can not even become a grave to great loves
        the house
           with honey-suckles
              dappled
           in the garden.

1930

POEMS OF TWENTY-ONE AND
TWENTY-TWO O'CLOCK

How lovely to remember you: among the tidings
Of death and victory,
In my cell,
And my life beyond its fortieth year . . .

How lovely to remember you:
Your hand lying forgotten on a blue sheen of cloth,
And in your hair the poised softness
Of the dear earth of Istanbul . . .
Like a second person
                    Throbs within me
The joy of loving you . . .

The smell staying at the tips of fingers
Is from geraniums,
A sunful ease,
The invitation of the flesh: a darkness,
                              deep
Warm, divided by red, bright rays of light . . .

How lovely to rememember you,
Write about you,
Lying on my back in jail,
Think of you:
The words you uttered at one place,
One day,
        not the words,
                but the universe in their tones . . .

How lovely to remember you.
I must carve something again out of wood
For you: a drawer,
A ring.
I must weve three or four yards of silk cloth,
Then, again, hurtling from my place,
Clutching the bars of my window,
I must shout to the milk-white
Azure of freedom the lines
I wrote for you . . .

How lovely to remember you: among the tidings
Of death and victory,
In my cell,
And my life beyond its fortieth year . . .

c. 1935

SINCE I WAS PUT . . .

translated by Taner Baybars

Since I was put in this hole
The earth has gone round ten times.
If you ask the Earth, it'll say,
       "don't mention it,
           such a microscopic amount of time."
If you ask me,
          "Ten years of my life."

The day I was imprisoned
      I had a small pencil
Which I used up in a week.
If you ask the pencil, it'll say,
      "My entire life time."
If you ask me, I'll say,
      "So what, only a week."

Osman, serving a sentence for murder
      when I first came to this hole,
      left after seven years and a half;
      enjoyed life outside a while
      then he came back for smuggling
      and left at the end of six months.
      Someone heard the news yesterday, he's married.
      He'll have a child come spring.

The children conceived
      the day I was put into this hole
are now celebrating their tenth year.
The foals born trembling on their thin,

long legs that very day
Must now be lazy
                mares shaking their wide rumps.
But the young olive shoots are still young,
        still growing.

They tell me new squares are built
                in my own town since I came here.
And my family in that little house
        is now living
            in a street I don't know
            in a house I can't see.

The bread was white as virgin cotton
the year I was put into this hole
and then it was rationed.
Here, in the cells,
            people killed each other
                    for handfuls of black crumbs.
Now things are a bit better
but the bread we eat has no taste.

The year I was put into this hole
                World War II hadn't started.
In the concentration camps of Dachau
the gas ovens hadn't been built.
The atom bomb had not exploded in Hiroshima.
Oh, time has just flown
            like the blood of a butchered baby.
Now that it's over
        the American dollar
        is already talking
        of a third World War . . .

All the same, the day is brighter now
        than before
                when I was thrown in this hole.
Since then
        my people have raised themselves
        half way up on their elbows.
The earth has gone round the sun
                ten times . . .
But I repeat with the same yearning
        what I wrote for my people
        ten years ago today:
"You are as plenty
        as the ants in the earth
        as the fish in the sea
        as the birds in the sky . . .
You may be cowardly or brave
        literate or illetrate,
    and since you are the makers
        or destroyers
                of all deeds,
only your adventures
        will be recorded in song."
The rest,
        such as my ten years' ordeal,
        is mere idle talk.

c. 1938

46

from *HUMAN LANDSCAPES FROM MY COUNTRY*

(The Night on August 26, from 2:30 A.M. to 3:30 A.M.)

. . .

2:30 A.M.

Kocatepe is a burnt old hill
no tree or song,
                    nor the smell of earth,
under the sun, during day
under the stars, at night
                    rocks
and in the dark now, ours
the world now in the dark, ours
and nearer,
          and smaller,
and because in such times from earth
and the heart, voices come to our loves,
our homes,
to us,
the sentinel with the homespun hat on the rock
caressing his moustache and smiling
was watching from Kocatepe (bighill)
                    the world's most star-lit darkness.
Enemy at three hours' distance
and if the Hederlik (badland) Hill weren't in between
Afyonkarahisar's lights would be visible.
In the northwest the Güzelim (my beautiful one) Mountains,
and on their hills dots by dots

47

fires are burning.

Akarçay (flowingbrook) on the plain like a glimmer

and in the sentinel with the homespun hat's reverie

there is now only

a voyage taken by water.

Akarçay maybe a stream

maybe a brook

maybe the tiniest river.

Akarçay, turning the mills at Dereboğazı (streamstrait),

along with the spineless needle fish,

enters and reemerges from the shadow of

Yedişahitler (sevenwitnesses) Rock,

and flows among the lilac

red,

white

flowers and with stems tall as one and half human beings

of opium poppies.

And, in front of Afyonkarahisar (opiumdarkcastle)

under the Altıgöz (sixeyes) Bridge,

bending to the east

and crossing the Konya railroad on the way,

leaving the village of Büyükçobanlar (bigshepherds) on the left

and the Kızılkilise (redchurch) on the right,

it continues.

Suddenly the man on the rock thought, of

all the rivers whose springs and wading spots were in enemy hands,

who knows how wide, how long they were?

He didn't know names of many. Only, before the Greeks and

Mobilization working as a handyman at the Selimşahlar (perfectsultans) Ranch

he used to cross at Manisa (Man-yssa) the waters of Gediz ('gean knee)

feeling dizzy.

Dots by dots

48

                    fires were burning
                        on the mountains,
and stars were so lit up and roomy
the man with the homespun hat
without knowing when and how it will come
believed in redeeming beautiful future days
and standing with his smiling moustache next to his mauser
suddenly saw him five steps from himself.*
Other pashas were behind Him.
He asked for the time,
The aides said "three."
He looked like a blond wolf
and his blue eyes flint.
He walked to the edge of the cliff,
bent, and stood . . .

if they'd let him
springing on his long, thin legs
and sliding like a star streaming in the dark
he would have leapt from Kocatepe (bighill) to the Plain of Afyon (opium).

1939-41 (written in Istanbul, Çankırı, and Bursa jails,
published posthumously in 1966.)

---

*The person referred to is Mustafa Kemal [Atatürk] during the War of Independence, which led to the establishment of the Turkish Republic in 1923.

NECİP FAZIL KISAKÜREK
(1904-1983)

Neither the sick wait for morning
Nor the tree for the martyr
Nor Satan for sin
As I wait for you

You dropped your shadow in my dreams
In my wet dreams
I drenched you
Now you may not return,
If you will.

1937

GAZEL

me, the odd visitor, of mysterious streets
escaping the echo of his own voice
me, carrying on his back, the unembroidered sin
the blindfolded it, of Allah, the sultan of djinns
me, the untiring landlord of empty inns
me, the endless forest for unwarmed arsonists
the polar sailboat towards pointed reefs
the orphan's golden fate against light on strings
me thought slipping through whose head is heavy
in the water mill of ego a blind long suffering ass,
me, mirror and dream, me whirlwind moth and candle
a miscreant corpse, dizzy, cunning chasm

1939

Merciful boxy hotel rooms, smoky oil lamps, oil lamps.
oh, my jisms of solitude.

. . .

1927

I am a wanderer on earth,
Moralists' constant misery;
Each soul has a haven, birth,
The world belongs to me.

Stealing with clownish pride every purse,
I lusted among the crowds for friends;
If dead, no one will follow my hearse,
the cursed corpse that it contains.

A new routine shapes up. I feel
No joy, nor ever sadden now;
Only brood over dreams I owned,
And pace my years from town to town.

FRET

A voice came out of elsewhere, "let this one
carry emptiness on his neck."
Then the roof suddenly flew off my head,
sky bend — trap within itself.

I ran to the red hell of the window.
What you'd said came out true, dear aunt.
Infinity, holding a blue lace,
shot an arrow from above, after my milk.

I tasted in this arrow poison of fire
into ashes an instant my diamond life
with emptiness nose-to-nose
I threw up myself.

The world is a glass of water
directionally fading emptiness folded
that's the honest truth and our dream
your wisdom and our drunkenness

Next, at my nape, a sledgehammer
I closed into my bed as a last resort
in the bloody dawn an anxious rooster
gifting me a new world

How's that? difficult to tell.

. . .

1955

54

SAİT FAİK (1906-1954)

THE MAN WHO DID CALISTHENICS*

I saw him from far. I wonder if he was around fifty. Along the shore where pieces of rock fragments had fallen to the sea, a pebble road rose gently to the clearing where he stood.

There were a few pine trees with the fresh greenness of sprouting thorns. I used to watch him do calisthenics there.

On my part, I lay on the rocks and daydreamed in the sun. One can trust daydreams in the sun, that they'll never turn out very badly. Yes: I thought of my woman, whom I'll never meet, and sang repeatedly to myself the song which begins with the line, "Time to use your knife now my woman."

First I wasn't curious at all. Everyone does calisthenics, nothing extraordinary in that. But if this continues for days . . . squatting and standing up, throwing his arms right left and above . . . then it becomes impossible not to watch him. As soon as I'd finish my daydreaming, and I would make out that the woman won't stab me, I turned my head left and caught him in his never-ending motions. The first few days he made errors in his exercise because of my looking at him; then, quickly and in anger, he turned his back to me. Anyone could hear him say, "How dare he watch me? Is it any of his business. . ." to himself, though none of us heard him. As he was uncomfortable, I looked more to spite him. For a while he tried to give up his cal-

---

*"The Man Who Did Callisthenics" takes place on one of The Isles of Prince, possibly Burgaz. By modern hovercraft about thirty minutes away from the city, the isles are still spaces of solitude in Istanbul. They were places of exile for Byzantine emperors, when deposed and their eyes gouged.

Sait Faik was gay. Before Ayhan, openly gay themes were taboo in Turkish literature.

isthenics; then he did the only sensible thing, ignoring me. He increased the pace of his motions.

He had an ugly body and had lost a good deal of his hair at the top. Since the distance between us was easily above four hundred meters, but not quite half a kilometer, I could see also the white curves of hair around his temples. "If he keeps on going like that, he'll give some real shape to his little paunch, black chestless body, gigantic ugly feet," I said to myself with an inner smile.

I have no idea about his face. Would I recognize him if I see him on a street? I don't think so, but if I see him in the village I surely would do so; and, if he does live in the village, I am certain he only leaves his house to do calisthenics. Would I not have met him around some place otherwise?

In the mornings, regardless of how early I go swimming, he is there. If this man does not arrive on the first boat, he is from our village. But, then, oh God, who is he?

I even thought of looking at him close by, even talking to him; but then I changed my mind. It would have been awkward. What could I say to him? "You are here morning to evening every day, doing your calisthenics. If calisthenics did anyone any good, you should have turned into something terrific by now; but you haven't changed a bit. You are even skinnier now. . . ." Is this what I was going to tell him?

The days went by, so did summer; and, even though I was curious, somehow, I didn't manage to get to see him up close. After his exercises, with a precision I almost could call chronometric, he tanned into black every part of his body, turning it to the sun, and then jumped into the water and swam frog-style quite far. He lay flat exactly ten minutes when he returned, and then, walking towards the rocks, he continued his exercises like a worshipper against the sun. The shriveled muscles of his arms shook, the hairless nipples of his chest rippled; and he didn't stop doing his calisthenics until I had gotten tired of looking at him several times.

When he joined his two legs straight and tightly together and bending rested his palms on the ground, I noticed something. This man had really beautiful legs. They were sinewy, thin and beautiful like a mare's. "Must be a foreigner," I said to myself. Among our folks you can't find men like that, and, if you find them, very rarely. Our legs grow crooked in our swaddling clothes. Even if not so, when you press them together, you always can see a whole panorama through.

I couldn't go to the swimming spot where he went for a while. I found other rocks and swam there. I relinquished myself to the sea, laziness, the sun. Unlike this other person, I didn't expect anything from the sea, or the sun. I only wanted the hours to go by. And among many other things, some evil, some sad events. . . . I was even trying not to think at all. But I knew that, visiting that place, I'd catch him doing his calisthenics, or blackening on a rock some last remnant of paleness on a part of his body.

It would be fair to say those days — last year — I didn't feel too much concern for this person. I was curious, but the passion to investigate, find out who he was, speak to him appeared only as a shadow on my mind. I only concluded that this man didn't live in our village, that he arrived on the first boat and returned on the last. I'd watched him for days, slightly patronizingly and mockingly, and then forgotten him.

And so the days passed. Summer went its away. If it hadn't, it would have gotten on our nerves. We already had missed the winter people, winter clothings, winter fruits, winter dinners. And winter didn't make us wait long. It came in three days. Going swimming three days before, "what's this cold?" we asked ourselves. We shut ourselves in coffee houses, got in and out of side-street taverns. We lost all our colors.

Not only unable to see each others' bodies, we were unable to imagine them. Then, suddenly, summer came back, of 1947. That summer I always went swimming to the spot where he'd also gone swimming. It is a solitary place. There a person can swim as he wishes, daydream as he wishes, and also, how should I put it, do calisthenics as he wishes. Yes, out of boredom, and sometimes out of pleasure, even I did some calisthenics.

Around noon time one day, I undressed under that green, short pine tree. Some people at a distance stopped and looked in my direction. I couldn't not pay attention to them and stopped my calisthenics. Sitting down on a large pebble, I thought. A man appeared. He was utterly bald, with a bulky neck, muscled shoulders. By his gestures, he didn't look like someone from our country. Before undressing, he sat on a rock and smoked a cigarette. Then slowly he walked towards the pine tree next to mine. He started to undress without looking at me and hadn't yet taken off his jacket and short-sleeved shirt when I recognized him as him. When for an instant he turned in my direction, I couldn't resist any longer:

"Is there no calisthenics this year?" I said.

He laughed.

"This year calisthenics finished." He said. "This year I lie down."

"You are," I asked, "a foreigner?"

"Me, Hungarian," he said.

Sitting down we talked. He stared at the dog next to me with distaste.

"Cats, cats, oh cats. Cats toujours good. Dogs no good. Dogs have bad ways, like people. Bad ways."

"How bad ways? Dogs are loyal."

"Loyal bad. What bad ways people have, dog takes. Donkey animal, no character. Cat is loyal. Cats scratch, they steal. Cat is character, big character."

He told me of the differences between cats and dogs, enumerated all the virtues of cats. He made such a list that I became practically unable to love my dog. Cats were pure. They possessed character, with personalities. They were ferocious. When treated badly, a cat did not act like a dog. Cats used their claws, were brave. . .

"Why not calisthenics this year?"

"Not calisthenics, because no enemies this year. Last year I heard bad words, I angry, but my body weak, will get kicked to hell. One summer . . . calisthenics! He told me bad things, so I hold him by the lapel and, 'Pan! Pan!'"

"Did you beat him?"

"Oh, yes. And how!"

He laughed like a kid. His blue eyes were telling in the way they showed how a person of serious character can become endearing. As we walked towards the water, he said,

"A real cat me, not dog."

1952

MARİCULA

I don't need paintings of women as in old dreams,
white and plump;
to me your teeth and tanned legs covered with bleached hair
on the beach are enough.

The dreams of smoky stations in winter . . .
coffee houses where we drink spiced wine
end . . .

You are nothing like the passion of insects in the color of strutting peococks
by the water,
or the torn underwear of children in the play ground running after each other;
the smell of cucumber in your teeth,
seeds of a tomato,
the purple's the rind
of a plum,
the smudge on your left cheek
by a slice of watermelon.

Maricula you'll fill up this shore
when you mend the fish net on your bare knees,
suddenly, you'll feel pain and lift belly . . .

They'll hail the boats, Maricula:
"Hey, captain, stop captain,
Maricula in labor,
every nine months and ten days,
with twins;
the boats are all ready empty,
waiting,
you can't catch fish alone, Maricula;

My future lovers with sinewy legs are in you!
Maricula, multiply, give birth, multiply Maricula!

1953

ASAF HÂLET ÇELEBİ (1907-1958)

The lover is only one, but to look at herself/
himself/
itself she/
it has put more than a
thousand mirrors before herself/
itself. In each
her face is visible
invisible.

1942

H

withhold the hoe
            oh! hi! o

who is two fountains for two eyes
            oh!

what is inside the horse?
the mountain sings
singapore inside you
            oh!

the dragon eyed it
two fountains for two eyes
flight flat under the feet

groaning and moaning
            private
            oh!

1942

UNCLE SEA BUOY

the naughty girl will come to the garden
to play with
the deadly buoy.

1940

MARIA

Dear as life
far as China
shut inside an atlas tinted Lisboa
one day you'll leave here
Maria
I search you in mirrors
liar!

smell of cinnamon
on your face
jinn*
in your eyes,
liar!
one day you'll leave here
liar!

1953

---

jinn: mischievous Islamic spirit; the etymological origin and a less domesticated version of *genie*.

A MANIFESTO OF THE EYE

I detach certain sound arabesques from their meanings and display them. What's more, even though these create an atmosphere, they are not without meaning either.

If the meaning of certain foreign words are realized, the reader fails to focus on the beauty of their form and melody.

A poem is nothing but a big word created by the bringing together of many words.

The pleasurable enunciation of certain magical formulas will be enough to open the gates of paradise of ancient Egypt, of Sufi mysticism, of a Byzantine church or of Buddhism.

If to these formulas, which are like beautiful animals, one adds only meaning, that is only intelligence, they become bad imitations of human nature and lose their animal beauty.

ORHAN VELİ KANIK (1914-1950)

"We wish it were possible to dump even language itself."
—Orhan Veli, from the introduction to *Garip* (*Strange*).

QUANTITATIVE*

I love beautiful women,
I also love working women;
But I love beautiful working women
More

*All the undated poems first appeared in the posthumous book, *Bütün Şiirleri* (1951).

MAKES ME DIZZY

Getting a letter makes me dizzy;
Drinking raki makes me dizzy;
Going on a trip makes me dizzy;
What's the meaning of all this, I don't know;
Someone singing "My Kazım"
In Üsküdar
Makes me dizzy.

1941

EXODUS I
translated by Talât Sait Halman

From his window overlooking the roofs
The harbor was in sight
Church bells
Tolled all day long.
From his beds the trains could be heard
From time to time
And at night.
He loved a girl
Who lived in the house across the street.
Be that as it may,
He left this town
And moved to another.

1941

My friend Sabri
And I always talk
In the street at night
And always drunk.
He always says,
"I'm late for home,"
And always two loaves
Of bread under his arm.

INVITATION
translated by Talât Sait Halman

I'm waiting.
Come when the weather is such
That there can be no turning back.

1941

THE GUEST

I was bored yesterday towards the evening.
Two packages of cigarettes didn't do me a thing;
Tried to write, no good either;
For the first time in years I played the violin,
Walked around,
Kibbitzed watching people play backgammon,
Sang songs off key,
Caught flies — a boxful.
Finally, damn it,
I came here to see you.

BIRDS TELL LIES

Do not listen, my coat, do not listen
To what the birds all telling you,
You are my confidante in life.

Do not listen, birds tell this lie
With every coming spring;
Do not listen, my coat, do not, ever!

1941

I AM LISTENING TO ISTANBUL

I am listening to Istanbul with my eyes closed
First a breeze is blowing
And leaves swaying
Slowly on the trees;
Far, far away the bells of the
Water carriers ringing,
I am listening to Istanbul with my eyes closed.

I am listening to Istanbul with my eyes closed
A bird is passing by,
Birds are passing by, screaming, screaming,
Fish nets being withdrawn in fishing weirs,
A woman's toe dabbling in water,
I am listening to Istanbul with my eyes closed.

I am listening,
The cool Grand Bazaar,
Mahmutpasha twittering
Full of pigeons,
Its vast courtyard,
Sounds of hammering from the docks,
In the summer breeze far, far away the odor of sweat,
I am listening.

I am listening to Istanbul with my eyes closed
The drunkenness of old times
In the wooden seaside villa with its deserted boat house
The roaring southwestern wind is trapped,
My thoughts are trapped
Listening to Istanbul with my eyes closed.

I am listening to Istanbul with my eyes closed
A coquette is passing by on the sidewalk,
Curses, songs, songs, passes;
Something is falling from your hand
To the ground,
It must be a rose.
I am listening to Istanbul with my eyes closed.

I am listening to Istanbul with my eyes closed
A bird is flying round your skirt;
I know if your forehead is hot or cold
Or your lips are wet or dry;
Or if a white moon is rising above the pistachio tree
My heart's fluttering tells me . . .
I am listening to Istanbul with my eyes closed.

1949

SUICIDE

I must die without telling anyone.
A drop of blood must be on one corner of my mouth.
Those who don't know me
Will say,
"No doubt he loved somebody."
Those who know me,
"Good for him. Poor man, he suffered a lot."
But the true reason must be none of that.

TRIP

Birch trees are beautiful.
Still
When we arrive
At the last stop
I prefer
Being a river
To being a birch tree.

PEOPLE

All the time
But particularly
When I know you don't love me,
I wish to see you
Like the people I saw
Sitting on my mother's lap
As a kid . . .

1941

THE SHAMEFUL FEELINGS OF A BAD MAN
translated by Jordan Davies

Every last girl thought my love poems were about her.
I've always felt terrible that it never was the case!

ECSTASY
translated by Gary Sullivan

Every woman on earth assumes
my love poems
are about her. I wrote them all,
it pains me to say,
in exquisite fits of boredom.

FOR THE HELL OF IT
translated by Talât Sait Halman

All the pretty women thought
The poems I wrote on love
Were meant for them.
And I always felt badly
About having written them
Just for the hell of it.

TO KEEP BUSY

The beautiful women thought
The love poems I wrote
Were about them,
And I always suffered
Knowing that I wrote them
To keep busy.

THE GALATA BRIDGE

Hanging out on the bridge
I watch all of you with pleasure.
Some of you are pulling the oars, whispering,
Some of you are picking oysters from the buoys,
Some of you are holding the rudders on the barges,
Some of you are ropemen at the hawsers;
Some of you are birds, flying like poets;
Some of you are fish, twinkling, twinkling;
Some of you are boats, some of you are floats,
Some of you are clouds, in the air,
Some of you are steamboats, dropping their smokestacks,
Like a rascal they go under the bridge;
Some of you are whistles, blowing;
Some of you are smoke, also blowing;
But all of you, all of you
All of you worry about a living.
Am I the only hedonist among you?
Don't worry, maybe one day
I'll also write a poem about you;
I'll make a few bucks.
I'll buy myself some food.

1949

THE PARADE OF LOVE

The first one was that slender, reedy girl,
I think now she's the wife of a merchant.
I wonder how fat she's grown.
But still I'd like to see her very much.
It isn't easy, first love.

. . . . goes up
. . . . we stood in the street
. . . . even though
. . . our names were written side by side on the walls
. . . . in the fire.

The third was Miss Münevver, she was older than me,
As I wrote and wrote and tossed letters into her garden
She was in stitches reading them.
Remembering those letters,
I feel ashamed, as though it were today.

The fourth was wild.
She used to tell me dirty stories.
One day she undressed in front of me.
Years have passed, I still can't forget it.
So many times it entered my dreams.

Let's skip the fifth and come to the sixth.
Her name was Nurünissa.
Oh, my beauty,
Oh, my brunette,
Oh, my lovely, lovely
Nurünissa!

The seventh was Aliye, a society woman,
But I couldn't appreciate her very much;
Like all society women
Everything depended on earrings and fur coats.

The eighth was more or less the same shit;
Look for honor in somebody else's wife,
But if asked of you to throw a tantrum,
Lies, fits;
Lying was second nature to her.

The name of the ninth was Ayten.
She was a belly dancer in a bar;
While working she was the slave of any man
But after work
She slept with whom she pleased.

The tenth grew smart
And left me.
She wasn't wrong either;
Making love is the business of the rich or the idle
Or the jobless;

If two hearts get together
The world is beautiful, it's true,
But two naked bodies
Belong in a bathtub.

The eleventh was a serious worker.
What else could she do?
She was a maid for a sadist;
Her name was Luxandra;

At night she would come to my room
And stay till morning.
She drank cognac, got drunk.
And before dawn, she went back to work.

Let's come to the last one.
I got attached to her
The way I loved no one else.
She wasn't only a woman, but a person.
Not foolishly after fancy manners,
Or greedy for goods and jewelry.
"If we are free," she said;
"If we are equal," she said.
She also knew how to love people
The way she loved living.

(This poem, which was found wrapped around his toothbrush after his death, is unfinished.)

CELÂL SİLAY (1914-1974)

. . .
branch swings in the wind
let it swing in the wind
branch swings in the wind
will swing in the wind
branch swings in the wind
could branch swing in the wind
swings in the wind
was was swinging in the wind
branch swings in the wind
must swing in the wind
swings swings in the wind
didn't branch swing in the wind
branch swings in the wind
let it swing in the wind
branch couldn't swing in the wind
branch swings in the wind
branch swings in the wind
wasn't swinging in the wind
branch branch swings in the wind
let let swing in the wind
couldn't swing in the wind
. . .

1965

OKTAY RİFAT (1914-1988)

ANCIENT SEALS
translated by Önder Otçu

All we do is read the ancient seals,
Shoot down warblers on the lioned road,
Over the mat that I meshed from equishaped rushes,
Against the mirrors with locked-in doors,
To lie, along with totems and leaving behind the wounded
Rein deer, morning, quarter past death,
While the carnivorous bird, unhurried, circling above,
Our corpses of ships and horses, cars,
Under the hurling rain of commas,
Setting out, trudging along, ever facing
the leaf, the weed, the star.
A fire all the day, a smoke all the night!

All we do is read the ancient seals,
Hunt down warblers and thus . . .

1969

MELİH CEVDET ANDAY
(1915-2002)

When Melih Cevdet Anday extends his range, he goes to the West;
when he explores Turkish themes, he remains on the surface.

THE PIGEON
translated by Talât Sait Halman

The applause that breaks out of the window.

BEHÇET NECATİGİL (1916-1979)

"where did Behçet Necatigil write his poems
he wrote them on medicine boxes"
—Cemal Süreya, 1984

In Behçet Necatigil's poetry words also get drunk and lose their direction.

EXAM

Written	oral	average
is good but	took a long time	wasn't enough
the next	took longer	time.
my right and left	emptying	was crowded
missing	to holiday	the heavy load
days	quickly	passed
unchanging	lists / lists	we stay
notes / are	broke	here and there
broken	with our leaving	we go sideways

1975

FROST

To our town this week
provincial newspaper
didn't come

those who come & go
time grows longer
the one who comes/become you

Was it beside
them
they came

with whom
they've forgotten
because they were too many.

Months year
dead fish in the lake
the poison you give a friend

year turned to year
someone look and find out
the one who comes/become you

1975

READY MADE

My body you are wearing, don't get mad, here, a proposition:
Mannequins in the window,
the latest fashion.

 Ask-
ance at emptiness, they are anxious and smiling
focused on time.
See, we don't
to care.

I know you can't choose,
but don't have to.
Like ma's boy
fast slashes of chalk and quick nips
they'll fit you up.

1975

92

HOUSE

Look, now, the table
Has found its place;
When we were not here
Someone entered my room.

The wash is done,
Everything is ironed;
When I had left
This book was on the floor.

You couldn't drink from this bottle,
Its bottom was so mossy;
It's unbelievable,
This is another bottle.

This old ladle
Is clean now;
Fire is burning
In the stove, our lamp is burning.

I wanted to hop into bed right away.
A ghostly presence
Came over me the moment
I touched the bed of feathers.

My wife must have dropped in
When we were away.

1953

UNSAID LOVE

You used to have a friend
About five years ago
I saw her yesterday
In the street. She was pleased.

Just there standing up
We said a few words.
She was married,
A girl and a boy.

She asked me about you.
"He hasn't changed a bit,"
I said. "As you knew him."
She understood.

She was happy. Loved her husband.
They owned their house now.
Like a criminal, guilty,
She sent you her regards.

1953

CAHİT KÜLEBİ (1917-1997)

Trucks carry melons;
I think always of her;
Trucks carry melons;
I think always of her

When the world changes,
Different water, different weather, different soil;
When the world changes,
Different water, different weather, different soil;

This city is different, I see;
Everybody fooled me;
This city is different, I see
Everybody fooled me.

Trucks carry melons;
I think always of her;
Trucks carry melons;
I think always of her.

1946

Rosy lips
your white hands
hold my hands, babe,
hold them a while.

In the village where I was born
no birch trees;
I pine for cool water, babe,
caress me a while.

In the village where I was born
no wheat stems,
toss your hair around, babe,
toss it around.

Where I was born
bandits prowl at night;
I hate loneliness, babe,
talk to me a while.

the village where I was born
only northern wind;
my lips are cracked, babe,
kiss them a while.

In the village where I was born
only sour faces;
I am shy and sad, babe,
make me laugh a while.

Your face like Anatolia is beautiful;
my village is beautiful too;
now you tell me about your village, babe,
tell me for a while.

İLHAN BERK (1918-)

from TIME OF HUNTING

I.

Tea Time

(*You! and tea time*) bringing the house to life. Halayık is pouring the tea. Lumps of sugar, lumps and lumps. Bedevi rewinds the clock. The Bey's slender penis slightly trembles. The castle gate squeaks. And a girl called Rage wakes up a girl, called Flower.

. . . and the Bey comes downstairs and kisses you. The house trembles slightly. And house gone.

The child lets go of his paper ship in the pool. Returns and waits for tea.

—

Your face sails far.

II.

Men

Men who went hunting are returning. They hold birds on their hands. Quietly the women waited for the men. Men return with flowers in their hands.

Swans look at the men returning from hunting. The hearths crackle. The women sit down and are read to from a book. Birds and flowers join. A peacock stands up as in a painting. A casement window opens from inside, closes from inside. And the Sultan's bootmaker fetches the Sultan's boots at last. Then they go hunting again. A man comes and teaches the women calculus (women knew mathematics then). A dog watches them and leaves. Then the cavalry soldiers come. Nobody thinks of the battle. There is only loneliness in battle. It can not enter any house. A Jew sits backwards at a student's desk and fucks. A girl looks at other girls. The man holds the woman's hands. The faces of the women were

long

a long

delicate

face

enters

paintings

There were no Americans then. Women wore underwear (Terry Moore visited Istanbul as Mr. Hilton's companion when the Hilton Hotel was opened and a newspaper photographer took her picture her knees up in bed with no underwear under her skirt. Oh, the scandal!). I began a moronic dirty tasteless poem, but couldn't finish it. Women were then in decorous paintings. Nobody went into houses. Nobody went hunting in the houses. But soldiers did return from hunting. But a book of tales always stood open. A window leaned against the sky,

(at which we used to look.)

. . .

1968

GARDEN
translated by Önder Otçu

Wall
Door
Window

+_____

HOME

"I am in the middle of a garden that looks like 444."

Cansever

The house, 'vertical creature.'
You enter the house through the garden.
But the garden does not know the house.
Nor perhaps the other way around . . .

How beautiful!
What's more, the world of objects is like this.
They all gather to enjoy the unknown.
The garden's choice has been freedom, from the very beginning.

It has the capacity of eclipsing the house,
however conspicuous the house might make itself to show off.

— I am in the garden, says the garden.

It has its own language, history, geography.

We have also come to realize that it has some peculiar thoughts of its own.
(Actually, it is through these peculiar thoughts that it takes shape.)

100

I SEE THE HOUSE AFTER I LEAVE THE GARDEN BEHIND.

To compare the garden and the house: the garden is wide open in the face of the close-mouthed, conservative quality the house characterizes (permeated with that despotism which wounded it long ago).

THE GARDEN DETESTS CALENDESTINE OPERATIONS.

Full of sound and voices.
Its face overflowing into the street.
Offering a female reading.

To compare them, it is sexual (what is not?)

THE HOUSE IS MORE AS IF TO DIE IN THAN TO LIVE IN.

Oh garden, the muddy singer of the street.

"Dirty Child."

Hello gardens, here I am!

. . .

1997

GARLIC

According to legend Asclepius brought garlic down to earth, rains creating it from the recipe in the dead Asclepius' hand. Born into the world so, garlic, Homer holding it by the hand, with him, became a citizen of the world. Since then, there is no place it doesn't get in or out of, respected everywhere. We know that during these journeys it has not changed much. Its head, always no bigger than to fit inside a closed fist, with a delicate, long stem, a long tail, it is smart, dignified and easy-going. It looks like an armed, caparisoned knight with multiple layers of clothing. And like medieval castles one must enter it through stone walls, suspension bridges, inner and outer courtyards, stone staircases, merlons, loopholes and towers. From outside it is like covered bazaars, musk shops selling heavy, pungent perfumes; looks like pitchers which let no water ooze; a sleepy church, its windows and doors shut, no light seeping out, no life. In its form it's pure, basic, not revealing its personality at first, in latent conflict. But if I take this, which is dignified, quiet and soberly withholds itself, this close box, if I hold it and pry loose its dry, dumb head with a few bites, stripping its first layer, then its second, then third, then its very thing, transparent membrane, touching once its tight, limpid white flesh, then how it will change suddenly turning into an monster, starting fires, starting screaming screaming as if coming to the world for the first time. Donning all its knighthood, its first words will be:

I ONLY EXIST BY MY SMELL!

And garlic is right to say that. What other earthly plant defines itself at first by its smell, that as soon as it announces its name, its smell is spreading? (I am aware as you are reading this essay on garlic you are experiencing that smell.) Doesn't Homer also, the expert on the aroma of meats, celebrate it first this way? Didn't in Henry IV's palace of domestic pleasure (where he assaulted women with garlic in his pocket) the court ladies know the presence of the king in the vicinity by the smell of garlic? What other vegetation's fame to such extent is part and parcel of its smell? Only the doctor of doctors Hippocretes and the scholar Ibn Sinai couldn't smell it, and they said:

EAT GARLIC IN THE MORNINGS!

What, what about Messegué, the great friend of garlic in our time, who said, "ON NEW YEAR'S EVE SEND EACH OF YOUR FRIENDS A SHEAF OF GARLIC?"

Of course, after securing its notoriority through these famous people, garlic rightly can, strutting with bouncing arms, enter the mouths of Gascony children and Fatih's, Sultan Beyazıt the Second's, Abdulhamit's and my kitchens, and, reassuming all its shy, dignified demeanor, land itself this way before me. That's how it goes!

1978

HOMER'S COMMENTATORS AND SLAVES

What kind of a guy was Homeros,
                    nobody knows whether he ever lived or died.

Homeros was tall, with a long, beautiful beard, says
                    Procles

and adds on the blind poet, "In the world
who saw more than Homer?"
one line
then he goes on and on talking about someone nobody heard of
    for pages.

                    What about Herodotus?

Herodotus, who always wore whites and only liked sea
    paintings,
    "Homer was from Smyrna," he says,
one phrase
    like Doric writing.

The Byzantine courtier Pavlos discusses him
    as an astrologer
    in one of his obscure poems
    which starts with, "On the silver plain
                    of his neck,"
    a poem which no more appears in anthologies
    (if one doesn't count mine).

As in ancient Aegean and ancient Lydia,
there are villages with still unknown names

Homeros is like those villages:
discovered, discovered and lost again.

Yet we know,
he never dropped him
                    from his hand, the atomist
Democritus.
And because slaves didn't know reading or writing
    they knew Homer
    And of the Republic of Alkinoos,
    mentioned in the *Odyssey*.

A commentary tells us that in the first editions of the *Iliad*,
discovered by Xenodotus of Ephesus, somewhere near Troy.

1978

READING LI PO

Sheep was the measure of wheat, cloth, tools
and gold:

1 Sheep: 40 drms. of wheat
                            20 yards of cloth
                            2 axes
                            3 grs. of gold

Then gold replaced wheat, cloth, tool,
                                    first cycle.
Then: "Paper money was seen in China," says Li Po.

    First tremor.

That day he let his beard grow, he let it grow.

1978

'NEITHER DID I SEE SUCH LOVES
NOR SUCH PARTINGS'

Each time I think of you
A gazelle jumps down, drinking
Water among the reeds.

Each evening a green olive
And a piece of sky take me
Boldly to your arms.

Each time I think of you
Roses grow at my fingers,
I give water to horses,
Loving the mountain more.

1955

JET-BLACK
translated by Önder Otçu

One should describe you starting from your mouth
Youngster, your mouth is silk from China, conflagrations, a jet-black amber

Your mouth, a spring of ice-cold water, a general strike
A foolish sea throwing itself from one place to another

Your mouth is that kid who sells dark blue-winged birds in the Grand Bazaar
It's a periodical titled Cornfield

These small, unpretentious rivers of ours are what your mouth is
Coming downhill a narrow street every day into a little square

Your mouth is "Time in Bursa City," shyly roofed flea markets
Night as written in the old Arabic

Kids, birds, summer times are all that your mouth is
Your mouth is a silken touch in my mind

1988

FISH MARKET, BACKSTAGE STREET

And so that the feet of the Sultan's horses are not sprained, all the streets of Pera were covered with rugs. And what about Eddie the Seventh, the Prince of Wales? In his visit to Istanbul, dear Prince had attended operas at Naum twice, the Sultan Abdul Aziz sitting next to him.

Which today is the mansion of Sıvacıoğlu, after this Salvo, the book store Sander, the patisserie Sembol, the shoe store D'Oree, which, I suppose, fed up being shoulder to shoulder with the hole in the wall slipper shop Martino at the tip of the street, seems always dour. The other old world denizen is the Italian restaurant Degustasyon next to the Arcade Hristaki (today, an empty lot, visited by the winds). And Degustasyon held Backstage once tightly by the hand. This is the true entry to the soul of Fish Market. And once you are in, first, flowers greet you, socks, slips, shirts, mussels, plums, cucumbers, tomatoes, thousand year old dried mackerels, blennies, plaice, Gregorian smells (do you know Gregorian smells? think of sea caves and a bit of salt and vinegar), Orthodox and Catholic faces, nylon and plastics, spices, clothing lines, tea cups, sheep lung kabobs, the Baptizer Yahya's wild honey, sour pomegranates, hair tints, sage, rue and flies and Galata rats (which are the size of cats and dogs and look at you in this wonderful, frightening way). And everything here is standing up: those passing or approaching to sit, those flying, those talking or keeping quiet, those loitering a few feet away — everything. And, then, as if everything suddenly dropped here out of the sky and will roar back in one instant to where it came from and disappear, in fact, as if sounds started a race among all languages and do not know how to stop.

Backstage Street here, in this world of sounds, suddenly strutting its arms left and right, hooks itself first to the Arcade Hristaki — which old folks called the Queen, and if there is a queen in the world, she must look something like her — then to the Crepin and the Arcade of Mirrors. Fish Market is these three-some, these triplets. Of course, to them we must add Backstage Street itself and

Duduoda and Nevizade Streets — these two historical relics.

On two feet the Arcade Hristaki today looks one foot in the grave, like buildings about to collapse. The inscription on a tilting rectangular plate points to the same thing:

FLOWER ARCADE REPAIRS
June 1, 1986

Proprietor: Niyazi Erol
Date of License: 26/5/1986

Whereas, once, Madame Iphigenie Espentos clothed the Sultan's harem here, stealing down fashions from Paris. The most beautiful shops are here. The Japanese Nakamura, short and looking at you with bleary bleary eyes and never seen sitting, exhibited his wares from Japan here. Nor did the young princes of the palace know how to leave his shop. Then, M. Perret? Who read up the French and English fashions daily? What a demon! The families of Bianci and Decugis, known never to leave their spots in front of mirrors, were clothed by him. And M. Paluka, undoubtedly the smartest dressed man of Pera, doesn't leave this shop. Only him? This is a place where every Pera family which is anybody waits in line. Today, the Arcade Hristaki resembles something which did not have those wonderful days in its past. As if the glittering world of this beautiful, four storey Neo-Baroque building wasn't a fact those days. Today, thinking on all those things, it keeps saying: "I died all kinds of deaths," maybe, keeps saying to itself, "I saw half of heaven." In this manner it is clinging, taking hold of memories. And who better than the Arcade Hristaki knows that being without memories is death. Then, fixing its eyes enviously on frozen times, Hristaki is thinking of the bar Sevic (which Osman Nihat, Salahattin Pınar and Ahmet Rasim considered their home), that's to say, of its owner M. Hacık (who was an aficinado of the hunt, but who, unlike our revered

Sultan Mehmet IV, didn't die in his bed but hunting), of Nektar, of Degustasyon, of Palmiye, of the Ankara beer house. Let's leave Arcade Hristaki to its thoughts. Finally, isn't history *an interrogation of the dead*?

And what of the denizens of this four storey, spiral building — till yesterday, didn't they maintain a regal life here? The Saras and Dirans of the third floor, the Iphigenies and Vartuhis of the fourth floor, the Nicolies, Luisas, Marias of the first floor? And these voices I hear now? Aren't they their voices?

THE DENIZENS OF THE ARCADE HRISTAKI

I don't love evenings anymore, said Diran, once I used to love evenings so much.

I don't want to recollect anything. Why should one?

Everything has changed, everything left its place to a silence.

Mari hasn't returned yet, said Iphigenie, Paluka must have closed his shop by now.

This Alba's tits are so big, said Vartuhi, and she is only fourteen.

She is like her mother, said Marta, once in Pera her breasts had no equal.

How many times I told you to have your hair cut by Izidor, said Armaniac, it is getting on my nerves.

Everything of yours, everything gets on my nerves.

How crowded Papillon the Accessories shop is, said Glavani, there is no way explaining women.

Memories made me fat, said Diran, I don't want to touch anything any more.

Looking out of the window is enough for me. There, Eleni is returning with her new blue bag.

She always wears high heeled shoes, she always goes out alone.

Pigmalion has changed its windows again, said Sara, stores don't know what to do.

What's eating you, said Martu, the whole day you keep talking like that.

What do you think? Don't you hear, they make love upstairs every night. That's what I am talking about, said Sara.

Then they drink Chinese tea till the evening, keep staring at the sky, I don't understand it.

The sky, which is ribbons, rag dolls, picture books, oranges from China.

This Luisa has reached her sixties, said Duran, she still can't keep her head out of the window.

Every night Lebon, Alkazar, Degustasion. She still hasn't had enough of the world.

On a 78 disc, every night, every night, Hafız Burhan, Osman Nihat, Hafız Cemal.

Lulu has become very forgetful, said Germaine, she is asking again how much water she should add to the pilaf.

She left the house yesterday to go to Shute's, she found herself at the church of Terre-Sainte.

We have become old, old, I can not pick two logs of wood from here to throw into the stove.

I told Yanni so many times to bring me dry wood, he doesn't understand.

I am burning all over for quite a while, I am trembling, said Eleni, the doctor is saying I've got nothing.

I should go to bed early, get up early, be careful not to catch cold, I should take care of my health.

I also told him I sometimes wake up as a butterfly. Such things happen.

Look, Sara has closed her windows, said Marta, she couldn't ever help thinking of her husband who sailed away on a banana boat.

How long Mademoisel Suzan's neck is, said Lulu, who does she look like?

Once she didn't give a damn about the world, she wore yellow socks and went to bed with whoever she pleased.

Ulla is shouting again from the third floor that she is going to Patisserie Markiz, said Diran.

To Markiz? said Madame Tilla, I never liked the smell of resin.

Returning from the Royal Hotel, I saw doctor Violi, said Eleni, he didn't recognize me.

He used to wave at me from Marta's window, he made me laugh a lot.

His house always smelled of carnation and oil. Among the smells of carnation and oil, I used to go and come.

For months now, said Armaniac, I don't want to go to Nektar, right under my nose. What happened to me?

Beyoğlu* has become a shroud now, no, is good vinegar!

See how night has come down, Diran said, we should shut the windows, night has arrived.

Night, now, everything is night, it has been so one or two hundred years, everything is night.

The world is full of loneliness, said Lulu, out of nowhere, I am watering the geraniums, I am changing clothes out of nowhere.

Oh, it doesn't end, said Armaniac, the stinking noise downstairs, these sounds of drums and fiddles.

I can't can't resist looking at Margarita's hat, umbrella, said Marco.

How she used to sit there before me and sang beautifully ballads from Tuscany.

Time doesn't know how to pass any more: children, trees, in water those who died in water.

Matilda's skin's smell, said Vartuhi, more than anything, I can not forget that smell.

Her silk stockings, especially her long legs, and her sleeping with a rose in her mouth the whole night.

And now, at four o'clock, I am tossing in my bed, keep tossing in it.

Beyoğlu: the entertainment area on the European side along İstiklal Caddesi in Istanbul

This world is strangling me, this house, this window, these curtains, this toothbrush.

This is Madame Anahit's accordion, said Matilda, I grew up with this accordion.

She is playing those lovely La Comparsitas, those tangos now to this ugly crowd.

I can't listen any more to her peasant tunes, to her onion smelling accordion.

This city, these bells, these sounds from the radio are driving me crazy.

How right you are, said Suzan, I don't want to see this Long Road, these trees, these people any more.

All together

Forgive us, all of you houses, streets, people, forgive us

Forgive us, old age, forgive us.

1990

ARİF DAMAR (1925-)

THE BROKEN SPOOL
translated by Simon Pettet & Murat Nemet-Nejat

Old friend, depart,
We climb the swings
of our silence,

apart from each other,
We swing, elbow to elbow,
stop,
then, by separate stairs,
return
to our thresholds.

It's evening,
We take the domesticity of evening
on our back,

In one hand the stick
on which we rest,
in the other,
disappearing daylight.

(As red in the western sky
strikes us to re-write fate,
sparks fly from our foreheads!).

It's evening,
We walk,
without dalliance,
We reach
the all-embracing sea,
kneeling,
We'll stay there.

First, we free our sweaty wrists
from the handcuffs
that old friend has fixed,
unawares —
unaware

the sea is tired.

And night!
Such night!
Rich night none can penetrate!

We part-open the door
Of the weary waters —

(In star light
We follow our light) —

enter in

"*Nothing in common*," she says
"—besides memories"
"*We've* nothing in common," I reply.

All that I might've gathered from *experience*?
ha! *tell me about it*!

If memories aren't *re*activated,
*re*experienced,
they wither and fade,
discarded, abandoned . . .

(*what other options had we?*)

We each remain silent.

And night
Such night
Rich night none can penetrate!

We don't look to the stars
nor pay attention to the sounds,
or to the silence,
We're ocean-tempered.

Night's pleasures
wait for us,
white water lilies,
waiting to spread their scent.

We're the curvilinear fantasy
of the placid lake,
its honest labor,
absence of pretension.

We're
the water lilies' unheard music,
echoing depth.

Tomorrow, together,
we might save the world,

but first, tonight, please,
may this night be over!

And night
Such night
Rich night none can penetrate!

That natural
undying loveliness
blossoms on the thinnest
of criss-crossing branches.

Let's break off, we said,

two filaments

                      of silver cord

pendant

                      in empty space

coming down

coming down

around

LOVE LETTER

After leaving you yesterday,
I went to Ilyas.
We sat down and talked about this marriage business at length.
His wife too said smart things.
I really like her, she said.
Who wouldn't want you to live together?
But she is not used to poverty
she can't really stand hunger or stripped down couches
As I listened I saw the poor woman was right
This thing between us seems impossible, what do you think?
You were raised this way by your elders,
always were served four square meals,
always wore watermelon sleeved summer dresses
your bed no doubt has springs
undoubtedly you go to one or two movies every week.
Life is expensive, i can't buy you shoes,
forget shoes, I can't buy you something to fill your stomach,
for example, I can't buy you books,
can't buy you a radio, can't buy you theatre tickets.
you are you, you'll go after many things,
I should tell you now, so that later you don't resent me.
i also smoke, drink raki,
there are folks I'm used to for years,
whom I believe in and love.
i can't do without seeing them.

Even if you accept all of them, how are we going to manage this
civil service isn't for me,
I am no good at business either.
That's how I am made.
Being out of shape I can't breaks stones either.
I am forced to make a living writing or drawing.
You will say, "Don't worry, my stupid,
don't worry." You had
once said, "I'll work if necessary,
I'll translate from English, I'll sew.
though I'm not strong enough to do manual labor.
My mother taught me all these . . ."
My mother too is a good woman you know,
sure won't act like a mother-in-law with you,
but she's sick, she can't do much.
Will you wash the dishes or will you translate books
will you sweep around or do your sewing;
this isn't one day, or five days,
once you lose your youth, you'll become bitter.
You know I also write poetry,
I use words like peace, freedom,
maybe some folks will resent these words,
will put a shaft into this beautiful activity,
I'll fall into jail houses, you all alone . . .

Before mailing this letter
I looked it over;
if I had other faults, be sure
I would have mentioned them too.

Now think, think it over.

1951

from THE ADDRESS OF TURKEY

VI.

. . .

"Only if this wick burns will the bottom of the pool enlighten," they said,
But neither the sparkle, nor the wick, nor the bottom;
They likened the lights of a deathly banquet to stain glasses in a villa;
Cross the threshold now, sweet basil leaves grazing your face,
Move round the burning smells of the pot, stray cats at your feet,
And don't hurt yourself for blowing too much on the wet sticks for fire . . .

And, then, turning round, press hard on the closed gate to withhold the vast
    terror of a sea,
Take shelter, in pretense, in the innocence of streets;
Ask for the drunken villa, peddlers of safety-pins'll tell you —
Even Hammurabi couldn't take such cruelty! —
False soldiers trim a handful of grass . . .

To find Turkey is easy, Turkey is the palm of your hand;
But you should tell its true place to no one;
Believe me they will laugh at you.

1965

124

A VIRTUOUS LADY'S UNFORTUNATE LIFE*

His name was Rüştü Pasha, was called Mad Rüştü in the Ottoman Army
Hamit was the Sultan then, his moustache long, long,

He had a beard, perhaps he was merely a beard,
Perhaps behind the beard a forest of a man

And the ships, like this, up the Bosporus, down,
My husband pasha twisted his moustache, without giving a damn

Everything flew by then, and we were so surprised
Freedom, then the parliament, then the thirty-first of March, then . . .

My sleep is fragments, I only wait for a call
You tell me, wise owl, when is dying coming, when . . .

I always looked up to something, defended it, was a girl
He was angry, had a harem, had a beard, he was my husband then

I remember one night at the top of the hill
Your weighty horses were Hungarian, my lace German

---

*One of the very few poems in the Second New written from the point of view of a woman. The poet chooses the Ottoman form of the gazel which by 1970 had become an archaic form. For poets writing in the 1990's, Ottoman artistic forms once again become a source of inspiration.

The naval chief Tevfik Pasha, the armistice, and Allah knows what else
How the world withdrew from under my feet then

A daughter, a son, two brides, one groom, Zurich, Lausanne,
How I cried after our house burned

I had not died yet, with my August and my pearls,
Before the night we visited our villa under a fulllit moon

When does my flower fade, when does the water, when the night
When were the ships, when my pasha husband, then . . .

Now only my aged glory could ease the glare of a chandelier
Tell me, the nights in my villa, when is Wise Death coming, when . . .

Elegies are read, waves wake behind a ship's stern
I am dead, Mrs. Chastity, from virtue's burn

1965

AHMET ARİF (1927-1991)*

"I am an easterner. I am not 'underdeveloped,' but I am a child of a country left intentionally back for the purposes of exploitation. I grew up with its customs."

—from an interview with Ahmet Arif in 1970

NOTES FROM THE DİYARBEKİR FORTRESS

I.

I can't bring myself;
When I can't resist her quinces or pomegranates
I bend my head
And walk away.
Nothing that wolves or birds can know.
Do not ask anything,
At all . . .
Let the dark decrees be sent to the roads,
Neighbors' gardens are all in ruins.
The fetlock draws blood.
After all what I have is a pinch of life,
All I can offer to this terror
By dying . . .
My hand is empty

---

*Ahmet Arif is a Kurd. The place he writes about are the mountains and villages in southeastern Anatolia, of which Diyarbekir is the capital city. His Turkish has the inflections and vocabulary of that region.

My foot in a noose.
Only I know
What bitch of a beauty I loved.
And she has a mouth but no tongue —
The Fortress of Diyarbekir . . .

II.

The fertile plants bloom,
Blood red.
It snows on the other side.
The Black Mountain rocks
The Zozan rocks . . .
Look, my whiskers are frozen,
And I am cold
And the ice has grown longer and longer
And I'm thinking of you, as though you were spring,
Of you, as though you were Diyarbekir,
To what, to what isn't it superior
The taste of thinking of you . . .

III.

The water of Hamravat has frozen
The ice is four-fingers thick on the Tigris
We draw water from the well as best as we can
We make our tea from the snow
My mother hides her sciatica like a secret
"Think of the wind" she sings, "and spring is over";
My sister is bearing a child,
She's very pretty,

You know her —
Her first. On the one hand,
She hides herself,
Ashamed,
While she's afraid of my dying.
Baby, where shall we hide you?
He is welcome
Right welcome
Ahmet Arif's nephew . . .

IV.

You were born
We kept you hungry
For three days,
We didn't give you your mother's nipples
Baby Adilosh
So you won't be sick
Because this is our custom,
Now attack the nipples,
Attack and grow . . .

These are
The rattlesnakes and scorpions
These have
Their eyes on our bread and food
Know them
Know them and grow
This is honor
Etched in our names
And this is patience
Seeped from oleanders

Grasp them
Grasp them and grow . . .

c. 1965

THIRTY-THREE BULLETS

This is the Mengene mountain.
When dawn creeps up on the Lake Van
This is the child of the Nimrod.
When dawn creeps up against the Nimrod
One side of you is avalanches, the Caucasian sky,
The other side is a rug, made of Persian stuff.
At mountain tops
Glaciers in bunches;
Fugitive pigeon at water-pools
And herds of deer
And partridge flocks.

Courage can't be denied.
In one-to-one combats they are unbeaten;
Servants of this area for a thousand years.
Here, how shall I start giving the news?
This is not a flock of cranes
Or a constellation in the sky,
It's a heart with thirty-three bullets,
Thirty-three rivers of blood,
Not flowing,
All calm in this lake in this mountain.

II.

A rabbit came up from the foot of the hill.
Its back pied,
Its belly sky-white,
A half-lived mountain rabbit.
Its heart so heaved to its mouth, poor thing,

It can draw repentance from a man.
It was solitary; it was a solitary time.
It was a perfect, naked morning.
One of the thirty-three looked,
In his body the void of hunger,
Hair and beard all mixed up,
Lice on his collar.
He looked and his arms were frozen,
This lad with a hellion's heart,
He looked once at the rabbit,
Then looked behind.
His unreliable carbine came to his mind,
His cushion wrinkled under him;
Then the young mare he brought from the plain of Harran came to his mind,
Her mane beaded blue,
Her ankles white,
Her cantering easy and generous.
How they had flown in front of Hozat!
If he were not now,
Helpless and tied like this,
The cold barrel of his gun behind him,
He could have gotten lost in these heights;
These mountains, friendly mountains know your worth.
Thank God, my hands will not put me to shame,
Will not shame the burning ashes of the tobacco
Or the tongue of the viper
Sparkling in the sun;
These eyes were not ambushed even once
By the ravines waiting for avalanches,
By the soft, snowy betrayal of cliffs,
These knowing eyes!
Helpless,
He was going to be hit.

The word was final.
The reptiles will cover his eyes,
The vultures darken his mind.

III.

In a solitary corner of the mountains
Among the hours of prayer in the morning
I lie
Stretched,
Long, bloody.

Hit,
I dream the darkness of night.
My fate is here,
My life gone before its time.
I can't fit it into words,
A pasha sent a coded message
And I am killed without words, without justice.

Dear guardian, write my story as it is;
Otherwise, they might call it a mere rumor.
These are not rosy bosoms,
But the dum-dum bullet of a barrel
Broken in my mouth.

IV.

They applied the decree of death,
Stained
The half-awakened wind of dawn

And the blue mist of the Nimrod
In blood.
They bivouacked our guns there,
Felt up our corpses,
Searched
My sash full of holes,
Took away my prayer beads and tobacco
And left.
These were all gifts to me from friends,
From Shiite hands.

We are mentors, relatives, tied by blood.
We exchanged with families
Across the river
Our daughters for years.
We are neighbors,
Shoulder to shoulder,
Our chickens mingle together.
Not out of stubborness,
But poverty,
We never got used to passports.
This is the guilt that kills us.
We end up
Being called
Bandits,
Killers,
Traitors.

Dear guardian, write my story as it is;
Otherwise, they might call it a rumor.
These are not rosy bosoms
But the dum-dum bullet of a barrel
Broken in my mouth.

V.

Hit me, bastards,
Hit me;
I do not die easily.
I am live under the ashes;
I have words in my belly
For those who understand.
My father gave his eyes in front of Urfa,
And gave his three brothers,
Three young trees,
Three pieces of mountain without their portion of life.
And when friends, guardians, kin
Met the French bullets
Out of towers, hills, minarets,
My young uncle Nazif,
Handsome,
Light,
Good horseman,
Hit brothers, he said,
Hit,
This is the day of honor
And reared his horse . . .

Dear Guardian, write my story as it is;
Otherwise, they might call it a rumor.
These are not rosy bosoms
But the dum-dum bullet of a barrel
Broken in my mouth.

1965

LEYLİ MY LEYLİ

. . .

It is the age, I can't resist it,
It is the age of your most
Intricate, rebellious, hell-budding
Body.
It is the age, forty nights and forty days
Your arms noosed around my neck,
And my heart, bent on evil . . .
What can I say?
When military patrols crush our sleep,
My heart is taken by you . . .
Your shadow even
Is forbidden on water pools.
. . .

I can not come down though your garden is in plunder,
My knife becomes as bright as hell,
Then you come down on me,
My hands are all broken . . .
. . .

In your secret, most private parts traps are set.
Some days I see you give up
The corrupting love of this world.
Some days,
You may fall.
Don't fall
Without me,

I will die . . .
I will miss your eyes, your eyes.
. . .

c. 1965

CEMAL SÜREYA (1931-1990)

HOURİ'S ROSE

I'm crying exactly in the middle of the rose
As I die every evening in the middle of the street
Not knowing my front from my back in the dark
As I sense, I sense the receding of your eyes
Which prop me up.

I hold back your hands, kiss them in the night
Your hands are white, again white, again white,
I'm afraid that your hands are so white
That a caboose in the station somewhat
I'm late at the station sometime

Palming the rose I'm rubbing it on my face
Which Houri dropped on the street,
My arms are broken, my wings,
In a red, catastrophic music,
At the other end of the reed
A brand new, gold toothed shyster.

1954

DYING IN A TURKISH BATH

Did you ever attend a public bath?
I did.
The candle near me blew out,
And I became blind.
The blue of the dome disappeared.

They relit a candle on the navel stone.
The marble was wiped clean.
I saw some of my face in it.
It was bad, something awful,
And I became blind.
I didn't expect quite this from my face.

Did you ever sob
While covered in soap?

1953

The woman stripped herself slowly,
Her shyness stripped her,
White and slowly
Without eye contact.

She didn't fetch her hair along,
Kept it on the dresser, full of despair;
But her hair fell through the unlit cracks,
I undid her drawers
I drowned myself in her hair.

She didn't bring her eyes along either,
So I only guessed her thoughts,
Her skin twitched
Like a rabbit's.

While a bypass
Is clearing
My upper plumbing,
A good lay
Is clearing
Her lower plumbing.

1953

The most beautiful woman, she was,
She combed her hair, all of it pubic hair,
When she sat, she squatted,
A bloody woman, a horse of wind,
It kept occuring to me how deceptive she was.

Which of her parts most? Of course, her mouth.
Attuned to all the feelings,
An Alhambra of a mixture of kisses,
In the limitless sea of the sheets
Her tactile mouth went up and down.

Oh, my eyes, now,
Have begun a crying that keeps on going,
A woman's shirt is shrouding me,
The blue of the day is on that
The rooster of the night is in that.

1957

Whereas a glass of water was enough to wet your hair,
A slice of bread, two olives to fill our stomachs
If I kissed you once, the second felt itself neglected,
If I kissed you twice, the third bent its neck in sadness . . .

1954

They sheared the cloud, the cloud now is clear;
My blood spills on the ground, the cloud is modest,
Blushes
And disappears.

A man's face shadows
In my palm;
I see it and squeeze it,
Drinking stars
From the urinal.

In a testy mood
The same mood that
Tore me apart.

His face is almost gone,
My desolation is pure,
The water is flat,
My pain is on.

1955

143

THE APPLE

You are eating an apple stripped naked
And the apple is an apple, nature's bounty,
One side of it red, the other side also red,
Birds are flying over you
There is a sky over your head
If I can remember it, you stripped yourself exactly three days ago,
On a wall,
On the one side, you are eating an apple, red,
On the other side, you are giving away your love for free, warm,
A wall in Istanbul.

I'm also naked but I'm not eating an apple
I have lost all appetite for such apples,
I saw too many apples, you can't believe it,
Birds are on my head, these are birds after your apple
There is sky on my head, this is the sky in your apple,
If I can remember it, we stripped ourselves together,
On a church,
On the one hand, I am tolling a bell to full living
On the other hand, people are passing in the street as a mob
On a church wall

A wall in Istanbul, a church wall
You are eating an apple stripped naked
You are eating an apple to the middle of the sea
You are eating an apple to the middle of my heart
On the one hand, our youths are in a profound sadness
On the other hand, the Sirkeci train terminal are full of men and women and
    children
Accustomed to letting only their mouths be kissed
Instead of doing their business standing up

I am dropping one letter from my name
The pimp dropping hints on the other side of the doorway

1956

THE BEE

You are watching a bee whizzing by in the room
The way
You ate your milk pudding
Three days ago.

Only after mere three days of my cajoling,
Coaxing, feeding, lying
You reached this serenity:
Thin, naked
Your pale, still unripe breasts showing,
Leaning against the board,
Nibbling a mackintosh apple . . .

1954

MUEZZIN

You hopped into bed,
But your hymen is on the table.
Never mind, Allah be praised.
There is more than one way to skin a cat.
Peel an orange and feed its slices to me.
I have a minaret, get hold of its charms,
Be my muezzin,
While the rain
Is pouring out in the street
And folks are keeping indoors
For their prayers.

1954

DRIZZLE

The stars were on the sidewalk
As if at the Prophet's coming
Because it had drizzled the night before
Dizzy like a cloud, I left her house
Skipping, skipping on the stars
Pleased as punch in the moonlight
Playing hopscotch
As at the Prophet's coming
Because it had drizzled the night before.

1953

Whenever we threw a smoke into the water
It kept burning til the morning.

1954

IN YOUR COUNTRY

The clock chimed: hmmm.
Bending my brim hat over my misery,
Out of my white insomnia,
Exile to your face,
You woman,
You were in every dark corner,
Your ghost nettled on the dead street,
A child
Sang lullabies endlessly, and a viola de
Gamba lengthened the blue smile of a young mother,
And you insisted on my love for your thin beauty,
My hope, a contention in abyss.

A lover possesses only his love,
And losing is harder than being lost,
Exile to your face, my woman!
I have not forgotten
Your eyes who are my brother,
Your forehead who is my child,
Your mouth who is my lover,
I have not forgotten your fingers
Who are my friends,
Your belly who is my wife,
Your front, your harlot's sides,
And your back,
And all these, all these, all these
I have not forgotten, how can I forget?

Strike a match, your voice flamed in blue,
Through the bright trees, your voice, the sounds of your tongue,

Into my mouth you poured, thickly,
The secret thoughts
Of this dour-skinned, this upside-down, this strange passion,
In your poison-dripping forest, gasping,
I lived your short, terrifying reign,
My heart was entangled with the tide of your hair,
And mixed, wanting,
With the Bird Sea,
Then mixed with the Black Sea,
Then with wider waters.

At night, the moon resurrects
The minarets,
Death flies with a somewhat beauty
Through hard, Koran-selling streets
(Death flies over child-soft faces),
I passed so many times
Through my streets
Your tongue's taste in my palate like sea-weeds,
Now misty, now blue-clear, now misty again
Like some sea-beings echoing some rabbits,
Echoing Mondays, echoing the other days,
Echoing Tuesday, Monday, Saturday and Wednesdays.

A stalk outbursts in miniature a city,
Down this stalk, round these streets, I press for you,
The world curbing circles, leaf by leaf, around you,
All thoughts of gold, the guilded coins,
And the right to press these coins,
The Euphrates,
And its sister river merging,
Dark circles in my eyes,

Trees of Babylon sapping,
The Sea of Marmara,
And the monsters in that water,
The sea crabs,
The land crabs, the sand crabs, the louse crabs,
Circling love crabs, the hermits, stoned barnacles,
Begonias, irises, castanets, all make towards you.

I who am a master in the art of complaining,
I feed with my life these falcons of sadness,
You whose alchemy, gnarled, I grasp and lose in the crowd,
Your thin waist
Drumming from here, from there,
In your lands where once joyful banquets reigned
Now big beaks of lonely hours are circling,
Now, please, once again, begin to undress
From your mouth,
Loose, once again, all your beasts upon me,
Once again, come rising from your ruins,
Come to me, once again, and disperse me.

1965

TWO THINGS*

Don't erase, my darling,
your sin
with your tears;
because sin is fertile;
it carries the indestructible
colors of terror
to dreams;
opening for itself
a dark path
it finds an abyss
in the purest water;
it trusts chaos;
its epithet is death;
even if the tree
rants in the burning hive
of the working bee,
its name is etched
in its trunk;
its leaves
will graze constellations
and the moon
will cool down
the cartilage
of fleet tense mares
don't try to erase it,
my darling,
sin is a knowledge
from day,

*Cemal Süreya was a Kurd also. Although Süreya was a key member of *The Second New* and Ahmet Arif kept out of poetic circles, they were friends. In subtle and deep ways they influenced on each other's work.

153

to the heart
to cancer.

In Sivas or in Malatya
I saw a child
his eyebrows arrived from far
and knitted together in the middle
in his teeth the longitude of poplars
I was just waking up
to say a few words
something suddenly happened
I don't know how
but the earth split
Did it say something?
did it concentrate on something?
In Sivas or in Malatya?
I looked around
leaves were turning the city to yellow
winter under the guise of autumn
was about to rule the plain
I looked around
a somber twilight was carrying
the sun's pack horses
from the paths
to the unshaven mountains.
Two things: love and poetry
both thrive on doubts,
as though something is missing
and there is still time.
. . .
Plato
because bargaining is a matter of knowledge
because screaming doesn't burst forth

from the . . .
but from the marrows
of orphans
like Fer . . .
impish, daring
don't try to erase it, my darling,
two things: love and poetry
one feeds on unhappiness,
the other on itself.

No help for either,
they grow.

1973

SECOND IS . . .

Second is the water fountain of eternity
If I only loved you like that

I have nothing left but the flowing street

That bird crawling on your back and your belly
And finally becoming a squirrel

Remember that young girl at the Afyon station
She had taken her shoes off getting on the train

The moon and I shared her legs
Her legs shared each other
and then parted
but I forgot her legs

Her legs shared the moonlight

I'd kissed her toes, toes, toes

Our prop was a paper handkerchief
If I had loved you only for that

A silver box was missing on the mantelpiece
If I had loved you only for that

We came to such a place
The sun, on!
The moon,
Moon!

Your life is seven lizards
Six have crawled away

1985

from COUPLETS

A tent at the skirt of a mountain
introducing nature to rooms

You generous September, the month of lights,
wait for us in the east, the city of curtains

The uncommitted looks of the earth without priority,
Crater lakes.

Those lakes saw nothing but
The sky.

Ankara, Ankara, my kind hearted step-mother*

In the past my first deed was to light a cigarette
now not to light

In every love there are at least ten people,
they are the nearest and dearest.

To deserve my grief
I turned back and walked miles

1988

---

*Ankara, the capital of modern Turkey, is a step-mother because Istanbul was historically the
capital city. Süreya lived many years in Ankara, as did Ahmet Arif.

PHOTOGRAPH

Three people at the station:

The man is sad
Sad like sad songs

The woman is beautiful
Beautiful like beautiful memories

The child
Sad like beautiful memories
Beautiful like sad songs

1988

Life is short
Birds are flying.

1989

This government
Doesn't give a passport
to Pir Sultan
I understand.

And doesn't give
Yunus Emre
a press card
I understand that too.

But this government
has issued a degree
doesn't let Karajaoğlan*
get on a bus.

1989

Yunus Emre, Pir Sultan and Karajaoğlan: three Turkish folk poets — all Süreya's predecessors whom he is saluting at the end of his life withing the framework of the 1980's political situation. The first two are poets of *Ilahi*'s, which are Sufi spirituals of divine love; they lived in the thirteenth and sixteenth centuries respectively. Karajaoğlan, who lived in the seventeenth century, is a poet of erotic love, the one maybe closest to Süreya.

"Dying?" you said.
"You're deep asleep in the bottom of a lake."
Seas?
The gods keep stirring up the seas.

1989

I'm dying, God.
This has happened too.

Every death is early death,
I know.
What's more, this life you are taking
Isn't bad . . .
No more said.

1990

After twelve P.M.
all drinks
are wine.

1990

MISS KINAR'S WATERS

She cried the smile of pebble stones with the raki from the carafe
from Miss Kinar now who became water to steep wells
with her straight hair what can she do in the theatre houses of Shehzadehbashi
she could not have enough hats

This bald Hassan, this baldie swept the darkness
his rebellious cigarette lit backwards to avoid any laughter
and a police enters fairy tales which go on ever since
parting the human eyelashes of children

And gathered inside her the sadness of the hands of an oud
playing woman, appeared suddenly into wells in the evenings crying
from Miss Kinar's waters.

1958

PHAETON

It is His Master's Voice, that thing being played on the record player
The anorexic melancholy of loneliness
As my sister passes by on a phaeton suicide black
In the streets of Pera in love with dying

Hysterical obviously my sister with gardensful of flowers
Freezes before a flower shop devoid of flowers
With only a gun from Karadag wrapped in indigo laces
And snapshots of hell and African violets in the windows

And I, refrainer from suicide the last three nights, can't know,
really, a suicide black phaeton flowing to the sky with its horses,
maybe, because my sister picked and bought the African violets from the
    windows

1958

TO TRACE FROM HEBREW

My legs are long
they are long wherever I go
wherever I go they find me
my sister in a blind alley

To trace a dove for this town
to trace the eyes of the dove
one dove
in the middle ages one dove with chalk

Along the whole wall trees cool
I am tracing a sound
I want everybody everybody to have a sound
in the dove a sound in the middle ages in my sister a sound

Wherever I go they are long
they find me from my legs always
as I trace a different voice
and a holiday full of flags in a city
in Hebrew

1956

WALL STREET

This walking reluctantly
pitch thought night hatless
a spiritual money exchange spinning out
sterling dollars, hard cash
cruising reluctantly this pervasive bruising

a whipped body's recline — against weeping willow
window sockets blind to this stretched pleasure
a rationale smoking why, stripped naked, stripped this body
was whipped up — glorified morning

I returning home
below sea level, a routed team
put back my lapin gloves into the closet
wiping my sole on the stoop before crossing in

tonight I shall propose your turn to beat me
a finite stretch of time the windows of Wall Street dark for eons —
infinity marries in mourning
my civil service pocket watch is running up

my lapin gloves must be returned

tonight convert symmetry into seduction
in this soft side street — walled street — my body will be fasting
this lemon moony skin deserves a good beating
without beating this lemon moon is not possible

a psychic omelet I'll

emerging out of reluctant infinitudes, crossing the threshhold
wiping my shoes on the stoop, hatless

1956

SPILL

then terrifying spill, smiles ended
then I saw nobody
everyone looking for me
a dead hungarian tight-rope-walker found me, found
me, the Sirocco was blowing from the sea.

1956

And the Sirocco was born
kneeling drew signs of peace on the doors
as much as I climbed dumb trees as a child
forgetting my objectives and subjunctives in the sea
reaching for bitter oranges, I became a bitter orange

1957

You have a smile, wicked, I'll grant you,
in your bourgeois slouch lipfuls of rose.

all your hands, streets of love, petroshka.

1958

MERMAID EFTALIA

Why, then, all too too long weekends bleeding into tuesdays
yet unholy Abraham is drowning in the brooks, circumsized
Richard Pryor is a lit match, running down the street
i don't see it, I, Isaac, for copper doors a copper knob
and mermaid Eftalia is petrified and holy, and floating like a log

This Istanbul so suddenly
is an itenerant comedy by a tubercular seal in the clouds
weekends jerking off and off, dancing the rumba, the rumba
on the organ grinder only, only the monkey grinder
my monkey back Eftalia, growing with her most ancient
silk hair expiring at her ankles, like her eyelashes
in her heart a welled sea-map, floating Eftalia

And lapping against walls greeting the hopeless Eftalia
hello hello hopelessly petrified cinder Eftalia
lullaby, now, good
bye weekends jerking off and off, dancing the rumba
the rumba

1956

A TREE FULL OF SONGS

I am thinking as a pandemonium, a terrible pandemonium,*
Saturdays coming to Turkish saturdays
Joseph wearing a hat and Josephs resembling him

Arriving, they are shouting a song, a panoramic song under the terrace,
on the swinging ass of Pilar and on these, these blind women

Lost in an Istanbul replete with Saturdays, you are imagining these songs
marching on the side of the union of prostitutes hiding from the republican
    reforms

really, you are not Turkish, but I can't quite remember
if you aren't, why are you a singer belting a song
on Pilar's gun burnt ass during popular sweet matinees?

in this pandemonium knowledge is willy nilly
in the secluded corner of the movie theater al-Qazar full of orphans, the vote
    of the peanut gallery doesn't count†

pursuing the darkness quickly you are tracing a tree of songs, prior to Joseph's
    resurrection
saw it chopped, branches full of holes

Pandemonium: The word suggests an illicit performance space in Turkish. Several references
in the poem are to the stage, theatrical scenes, and actors. Saturday is the matinee days for kids to
go to the movies. A tree of songs is analogous to a stage prop, a tree with songs instead of real
leaves.

†*al-Qazar:* a movie theater in the Galata section of Istanbul. It used to show many action movies
in the 1950's when this poem was written; therefore it attracted kids during the Saturday
matinees. It also attracted sexual predators: that's why, "full of orphans."

let us not cry, a tree full of songs
think of us, of children of al-Qazar without weeping, a thrush of songs.

1957

HARBOR

Bottomless wells of mother's grief
Galata has lost two wild
and crazy boys
their legs rumored wandering on the piers.

At the crossing of the vernal equinox
because the two kids are taking a break
will oversleep
and miss it.

1959

THE NIGGER IN A PHOTOGRAPH*

Accursed. The curse which with its curving unsheathed letter will never leave me alone, which I take everywhere, my invisible dog, the curse. Who can be friends with me? Who? It is said that I carry that monk's blood, and with a relentless agitation I run here and there, barefoot, and on my tiny chin a big beauty spot, I am known with my covered beauty still. Like the stain in the curve of the letter U.

Flower. I began my adventures as a flower vender. Flowers and children bedecking a string, dry petals. But how I was under a spell those days. Because of a little fairy's curse, I couldn't be looked at. Light Maltese fevers run in empty lots in summer evenings. And endless hallucinations full of clowns run in ruins. Then a stone arched passage. I am living in the drawer of a fifty-year-old witch, nailed. Am I really? One can not tell what season it is, and I am cold. Curved like the letter U.

. . . went to Jerusalem in that exile of the flower vendors and got settled in the town clock . . . But to remember these things, I don't want to remember them. . . . It had run out, the money I had saved selling flowers. . . . This far away from Smyrna, I was pawned. Let this be the nigger in the negative of a photograph from me, will you receive it one day? I had it taken while learning Hebrew, with my invisible dog inside a Jewess. Lonely and terrible. Under a huge tree which had shed its leaves, barely touching a chair.

It is not out of pity, but I am worried it won't pass. The curve of the letter U.

1965

---

*The poem is the opening piece of Ayhan's second book, *A Blind Cat Black*. The book is has the evocativeness of a children's fairy tale. It also tells the story of a boy seduced and turned into a hustler.

EPITAFIO

They came drowned in the afternoon to the blue house on the wharf of brown broadcloth cafés. Her fate was in Spanish.

They are bending their heads again, for their sister, as in the morning. She promised. She will comb their hair and part it in the middle. The deadtangle.

And it is calling them, screaming, screaming, from an alley of card players, a children's game with thousands. The jack is up.

They see it and how they laugh with their enduring chuckles. But they can't join the game. What can one do? Their bundles are being wrapped. They are in a hurry. Rotten . . .

Will she appear again before them the fat woman who wants the hooks and eyes of her winter coat to be clasped, and their sister, also, on the mossy rocky road to Africa?

1965

ORTHODOXIES I

His only side — his face — to be talked about: the space between his legs. And he has grown a moustache and a beard. An inveterate. A pervert. Such talk about him. He doesn't go near women as he should. He whets suspicion. An erect plume on his head. A pornographic masterpiece. He is buried alive in the ground. Head first. Ouch! A few sail boats, startled, shine at a distance. Why couldn't I understand?

Modesty, a mood. Shame is led in delicately by the hand. A girl, blighted. Walks under the eaves of her man. The door locks have given in by themselves. A shroud moves. She has grown pregnant by leaning over the corpse. Which pretends impotence in a church. Before it grows. She has reared the foundling in the marshes. I was burning a blank letter by pouring gasoline on it. A con man's envelope on the sidewalk. Shining beeswax. Melts.

Now, a leftover. Know. The bend in a child's heart. His crafty, elegant wrist. And how he holds a hawk, stuffed, whole, trying to preen its feathers. He has writings etched over his breast in saffron repeating, embroidering one word from the lexicon endlessly: hermaphrodite. A hermetic woman. A man and a woman. She makes love biting his own lip. He plays the hand-me-down tune on the lute. Of the scared. I was reading *The Jew of Malta*. I took shelter in a coffin.

1968

ORTHODOXIES X

The last fast day in a leap year. Beginning night hours. Abstinence. Vows of silence. The suckerandgusher black pump fell quiet. Now a gray whisper, asked, "who is it?"

1968

ORTHODOXIES XV

A crack of lilacs. A mask chipped off their wood. It is impenetrably wide, he understands.

Kneeling, he groans, one Benjamin. Weaned off the smell of armpits. A cup of hemlock not left around against the possibility of drink.

And there is a majolica on the mat. A fortress tower rings, of the harem's eunuches, washed in the flood.

Screaming, under a parasol, he adorns the portable throne. In a blackout. In his birthday suit.

And a slut is giving him a broken tipped sword. Reveals herself on the rung of a ladder. Oh, Benjamin!

Two snakes entwined, trajectories melting away at an inn. Turned around by so many bends.

In the guise of an eagle owl, bubo-bubo, the fallen Christ goes out to paint the town red. And he won't come back.*

1968

---

*The Russian Orthodox belief that, in the shape of a beggar, Christ will cross Russia one day. The Russians wait for him. He wanders now in the cities at night disguised as a large owl, "bubo-bubo."

GÜLTAN AKIN (1933-)

THE WEDDING AND THE SNOW
translated by Önder Otçu

A mere wedding's sadness, warm, diaphanous,
touched the densely falling snow
of the dense silent evening.
So the two saw us off with sweet goodbyes,
the little girl, the young woman,
and all the rest were inside
and all along the street
us alone

snow on my chest, you knee-deep in it,
your white wool shawl wrapped around your neck,
we walked,
all the rest were inside, there,
was it that they were foundlings lucky to . . .
or that winter night, were they so tied
to soft beds in warm rooms
that they found

As the snow grew upon our feet
too heavy then to carry along
were we frozen
trudging uphill

up to the swing-door
where we paused and wept
all in each other

so tranquil, and even softer,
made as though from fine threads of silk
restrained yet a bit crazy
achy breaky a bit
bringing together the farthest ends, overjoyed,
yet standing so nobly calm

followed by the work of death
is this insurmountable wall now
the type that rises higher with pain,
in the nights of snow to follow
burnt by the yearning,
Alone I kept
walking.

1998

ÖZDEMİR İNCE (1936-)

SAGE

translated by Simon Pettet & Ülker İnce

My dreams! you used to say
my dreams shouldn't frighten you
but you should also be aware of the world.

As if!
I'd said it all
but all the words had erased themselves.

As if!
I'd seen it all, even the most arcane revelations
but they had been shrouded in darkness.

As if!
I'd heard it all, even the sounds beyond sound,
but had forgotten all the images.

As if!
I'd walked all the roads in vain
realizing that none of them leads anywhere.

As if!
Two armies had attacked each other
and inside my body only a scream remains.

As if!
I'd filled a jug of water and taken a handful of soil
from the shadow of the sea and the earth.

O then I become a wind that had once blown
a flood that had overflown
a rain that had rained down.

My dreams! you used to say
my dreams shouldn't frighten you:
Death never kills anyone!

1991

1968, FILLED WITH LOVE

The nickel you found on the sidewalk with the corroded head and tail
the broken glass the sea threw on the shore
the engagement ring too tight on my finger
the linen shirt with buttons missing
the exercise book turned fragile and yellow

a manuscript left in a used-books store
and the tune in the Huzzam mode radiating from a house
returning from a drinking binge one evening

a father's inheritance of markers to be paid

Casa Caramina Sierra Maestra and Maspero
old tapes sounding like cinnamon
asphalt roads hiding cobblestones
yuppy revolutionaries in parkas
children of fairy tales

the piece of good luck you found in the open sea

1991

STAY WITH ME

Stay with me finally
as my son's smile
as *much as* my son's smile,
stay with me now
as my son's shadow
as much as my son's shadow,
stay with me more
as my son's voice
as much as my son's voice,
stay with me endlessly
as my son's stare
as my son stares,
stay with me mirage
as my son's odor
as my son's odor.

. . .

1990

CONTINUITIES

they call the waiter with a camel's bell
and have a threshing machine
turned upside down — columns of carved stone underneath
make a table.

The bell rings, bell ringing
the water turning to fire.

the water turning to fire in my blood
you have let yourself to a current
which takes you from the bottom
to the source — torrential —
with trees and fish

"How did you arrive here?"
if they ask you
will you say, "I saw water turn to fire?"
or will you point to the forest fire?

Do you know? "I have only one life to live,"
I am saying to myself,
under the sun where
there's nothing new under
only one life
and it hasn't begun yet:
looking for overalls and fetters for your wind

That's how things are . . . that's how they are:
One doesn't see water turn to fire
and one calls the waiter with a camel's bell

1990

MELİSA GÜRPINAR (1941-)

THE BANK TELLER TECELLI BEY*

The bank teller Tecelli Bey
greeted his mother-in-law,
who was sorting
string beans
under the chestnut tree,
with his head.
Only nodded his head
and, with his son,
walked past her.
His mother-in-law,
seeing her in-law, with a mysterious intuition
checked if her money was in its place
in her sock,
and her eyes caught the white roses
that kept blooming since the day she'd left
the Palace as a bride,
the white roses which had the look of a wandering
dervish, whose branches hadn't
been pruned this year, and

---

*The Bank Teller Tecelli Bey: Attitudes in the poem needs to be understood in terms of social relationships. Tecelli Bey is a "house groom." Being socially and economically inferior, at his marriage he had to move into his wife's household, which had connections with the Ottoman court. The mother-in-law's contempt for him derives from it. This is an emasculating reversal of social order, reflecting the reversal of order in Istanbul itself.

the apricot tree
wasn't lime-washed
this year, and thieves
were constantly stealing the gutters,
stealing the zinc falling from the roof in broad daylight . . .
lavenders, boxwoods had overspread their branches,
but her son-in-law didn't care,
knew only how to go to soccer games with his son,

"What is it about this Fener-
                              Bahçe *
stadium?"

In his sixties the man was living in a globe of ice,
if one asked her
can he be of use to anyone a man who drinks
a bottle of Marmara wine every evening
to the tune of poached blue fish smoked in cardboard ?

As the mother-in-law
sorted the string beans, first dividing them with her hand in half,
who knows what else she was sorting in her head as best as she could?
"I wouldn't sell this villa in its time,
wouldn't I to leave it to this awful man?
Oh, what a head!"

---

*Fenerbahçe: The soccer team in Istanbul with most fans from the working class, *Galatasaray* being the team of the intelligentsia. *Fenerbahçe* is made of the words *Fener* (lighthouse) and *bahçe* (garden) and is also a neighborhood on the Asian side of Istanbul; *Galatasaray* has the word *Galata* in it, the district of the minorities on the European side. The poem implicitly refers to the Istanbul of the 1960's and earlier — and the psychic structure of *The Second New* — the loss of which it mourns.

Gürpinar's use of *Fenerbahçe* has a touch of Ayhan's punning. The aristocratic Ottoman garden of the mother-in-law degenerates into the populist soccer team in the retarded grandson. The power of the poem is partly due to its wobbly perspective, which includes both the mother-in-law's and Tecelli Bey's.

Every time she shook her head,
hair pins slipped from her white bun, fell on the flagstones . . .

The white roses shook gently to both sides with the off-shore breeze;
The garden gate with the bell opened and closed.
Two boys dove fast into the garden.
"Granny, give us sugar."
In the mother-in-law's pocket there were always a few caramel drops.
She made the children read the fortunes
wrapped around them.
"Eat the insides," she told them, "they stick to my teeth";
anyway, her false teeth were ready to fall off,
nothing sticky pulling them down,
whereas in the cabinet next to her bed, always locked up,
she kept hard, Akide candies

                    (Akide Bey,
steward of the Sultan, licensed
producer of royal candies)

"but even if she didn't lock the drawers
who would eat those old fashioned slowly dreaming melting-in-your-mouth
    candies?"

she wandered . . .

The petals of the white roses
had tinges of yellow and pink,
the season for roses is past,
but even if they lose their scents and colors,
the seeds she brought from the palace insist on blooming . . .
sprout under the snow,

the buds at the tips of naked branches stand erect and proud,
as for lilies, they are in the bud,
if the chestnut tree gives plenty of chestnuts this year,
the mother-in-law will hire extra hands
to haul the chestnuts inside the house
before the quilt-maker's apprentices
swoop over the tree . . .

The bank teller Tecelli Bey
held the hand of his thirty-five year old son,
who was lame and stuttered,
injured at birth
people said,
that is also why
he's retarded,
his father mistreated the indentured servant girl
of the house
other neighbors said,
and look what happened to him . . .

there was so little to talk about
and time was passing so quickly,
it had been forty years since Tecelli Bey walked in as a groom to this house,
his wife or mother-in-law
didn't listen to him even for one day,
his father-in-law had long passed away,
he was a graceful civil servant from Istanbul,
who was appointed Secretary to the new parliament in Ankara,
and under a flag wrapped as gracefully around a coffin
he had returned to Istanbul in two years,
no more children necessary, his wife and mother-in-law said,
and Tecelli Bey poured all his love on this child,

went to soccer games with his child,
lay on mats on the floor and solved crossword puzzles . . .
and late Junes, in his pajamas
drank wine on the terrace,
watched glow worms,
loved beans with chopped scallions, meatballs steeped in vinegar, semolina
    cinnamon puddings,
it isn't quite clear what he thought of Hitler . . .

His stocky and reedy voiced wife
leaves the carafe with the ice water next to him
and walks away quietly . . .

Everyone seemed to talk silently,
is startled when they hear loud laughter from the tenant in the basement;
thank God,
mother-in-law never turns off the large voice box in the reception room,
radio is the voice of the house,
she says,
and at midnight, obviously, the rats in the attic are the voice of the house,
at noon the roosters, and the sound of the-sucker-and-gusher pump is also a
    voice,
the wind-mill over the well creaks away . . .

Some days, setting his cart outside the garden gate,
the taffy vendor sang gazels . . .
The rest was all soundlessness.

Tecelli Bey inspects what his son is wearing one last time.
Clothed with care, he should lack nothing,
his knickerbockers, his linen hat . . . perfect

In his loose and zippered jacket, Tecelli Bey
walked in a dream, dragging his feet . . .

and he always left something back in the house,
and this time his tobacco bag on the stool,
"ah," he says, "ah,
retirement did this to me . . ."

if I leave these two women for a few days
and find my ancestral house in Kır

                Şehir,

maybe . . .

if one becomes the house groom in a rich man's villa in Istanbul,
it's like this, one loses everything in forty years . . .
the road was extending achingly . . .

his son is biting his own hand,
bitching,   all the way,
      belly-aching

"Dad, buy me the Team Flag."

1990

ENİS BATUR (1952-)

GLORIA*
translated by Clifford Endres & Selhan Savcıgil

"The root of the problem, I think, is that we've lost
Cicero's *Gloria* anyway, Petrarch read it before
he wrote that smart-ass *Epistolia*." The old poet gets up
and for the umpteenth time opens the window to air
the low-ceilinged room chocked with cigarette smoke.
The other slowly perks up: by his manner you can tell
he's of an age that still believes the night is not bottomless:
"*The Vita do Dante* puts it perfectly: the guy's a fool for fame
obviously, don't be taken in by the *Purgatorio*'s clever posing,
he blurts it out — *grido, rumore, nominanza, onore* — he's
trying to say these words are empty, but deep inside
he thrills to the thought of wearing the crown."
And so the tempest passes. The old poet feels relieved,
those letters dashed off in Barcelona to a prospective translator,
that bit of lobbying before the prize, dissolve like mist.
They're quiet a while. All at once between them there's a feeling,
as if behind the door were someone who could hear.

1990

Gloria: This poem and the following, "Passport," belong to *The Gray Divan.* "Divan" is a
collection of poems by a poet in Ottoman or Persian literature; it also refers to the total body of a
poet's work. Using the word, Enis Batur is making a connective gesture towards Ottoman
literature.

PASSPORT

Aunt Aagoni died in 78, my great uncle became quiet then, for an old man
to be alone is difficult, the year I went to law school
I went to see him first, my mom had sent dates
and a sweater — now was living in a single room, that house
on Tomtom Street doesn't leave my eyes, wasn't dirty, no, rather, one
could talk of an infinite vagrancy, all ready
to depart, in truth, for a place he was
late for for years.

Passport.
162938
KINGDOM OF EGYPT
no. of passport 36424
Name of Bearer   Armenag Shaheniantz
National Status   Egyptian Subject
Profession   Sales Manager
Place and date of birth   Baghdad, 1904
Domicile   Cairo
Height   171 cms.
Colour of Eyes   Brown
Colour of Hair   Black
Countries for which this passport is valid   Palestine
The validity of this passport expires   4th January 1934
unless renewed.

issued at Cairo
Date 5.1.1933

I tried conversation naturally, but as you know
beyond a certain age the weave of thought
becomes tangled, with what passes his mind at that moment
and the confined slice of the past getting mixed up, and from a system
whose logic only *they* could see, hallucinations were rising,*
words, and a few signs.
He was fixated on Eastman's suicide, had heard the news
in 32 when he had started working as Kodak's
representative in Beirut, *they* couldn't still comprehend
it, how could an old man turn away
from life.
He also kept saying how on December 9, 1936, he came
to Istanbul. it was a magical date
in his long migration — without him ever,
ever intending really to stay for good. Then, the enthroning of King
Farouk in Egypt, those days
in the Middle East everything was uncertain,
uncertain.
The Peele report, the hangings, hundreds of Jews and
Arabs died in the rebellion, I think also quite a few
English, the Mercedez gifted by Hitler, Kodak's
system of management full of indecisions . . .
That place wasn't for my great uncle. Your passport points to the same thing:
neither his place of birth Baghdad, nor Cairo or Beirut
where he blew, nor the place of return Istanbul,
where he settled, could contain
his migrating body. He fell as a stranger
on earth, left the same.

---

from a system whose logic only they *could see, hallucinations were rising:* This is a narrative
whose center is *they* (the fluid unity of 'I,' 'you,' and 'it' in *eda*).

In his 1908 essay, *Poetic Creativity and Daydreaming*, on the surface
plain as a piece of dunked bread in water, for the first time
Freud pulls in child and poet in the slip-up expression
of play, the child in his play, the poet
in his writing, the neurotic
in speech release
an energy potential the ordinary mind silences
or suppresses, they are blocked
and locked.

"How possible," he says, "forget about expression,
a poet can sense and relay certain feelings and sensations
which we wouldn't hope to recognize
even if we encountered them,
giving us the key towards the end of the essay:
"The technique that in essence embodies
ars poetica consists in the crossing of the limits, splits
the hesitations which exist between
every "i" and the other "i"s. This is
technique's essential function.

Along with very first pieces, the mother lode of anxiety
which accompanied them turned contradictorily
into the main engine. In reality, I had
a considerable stock of experience behind me
to enable me to move from a poetics high in abstraction
to a poetics high in narration: in an arc
starting with *The Tropic of Scorpio* to
Fugue, I'd both used narrative techniques and
developed spectacles. Still, the poems in *The Gray Divan*
constantly provided for me tortuous issues
of equilibrium between romanesque and dramatic

factors. As Freud's concept of floating fantasy space,
completely on the nose in my opinion, interacted and was
fed by the gap between i and the other i's
also in the same essay, on the one hand, the process of writing was getting
        more and more
complex, on the other hand, the very same process
was creating the poem.

Ah, if only the floating time curve which breaks out of its focus in the present*
to the past or to an indefinite, desired point in the future
weaving back and forth, could limit, restrain itself to the I
writing the poem! but the i's who are the subjects of the poem are
introducing their own arc before me, besides, the subject of the poem.
is not always I, I though whichever space
I place myself — even sometimes beyond — it was always I writing the poem
My own fantasies and those I loaded on other i's, and sometimes
filtered became passages in one single
labyrinth.

From one end to the other, with its various sequencing,
can it be said that *The Gray Divan* still embodies a novelistic structure?

Emptying the bottom drawer of the dresser in the bedroom
they gave it to Vahan Bey: a roll of letters
wrapped in nylon and tied with plastic,
full of calculations — now meaningless — a notebook,

The floating time curve: the weaving of past and present into one continuum, which is the Sufi
essence of time. In this perception the splits between past, present and even future disappear into
a simultaneity — into movements of perception.

Passport is not a 'Freudian' interpretation of a Turkish philosophical and poetic process;
rather, the reverse, a Sufi take on and a re-framing of a Western European icon. A centuries old
trend is reversed. This is the importance of the precedence of *East* in the title of Batur's book,
The East-West Divan.

the passport and the folder of Chamber of Commerce
file came from there. I know that house
on Tomtom Street: just down the Spaniards',
attached to the garden, a two-storey ruin, the front faces
the Palace of Justice, on one side
is the Italian Consulate — to me a dark, strange
lake with various registers of depth, when I go
down the street, reaching a certain point, a light
flashes from the small bell of the church, though I have no prayer
to say, the place I'll pray is either on the tongue,
I descend slowly with a foreign sadness which, how could I know,
lived in that place, even if I did, what
difference. — Vahan Bey has spread
the flyers of the bank on the counter,
a few old movie posters, a pile of magazine issues serializing
The Juif Errant with illustrations is visible, next to some photographs, this
          antique civil servant discussing
seriously, in detail, the fine points of Bozcaada wines
with a friend, his coin purse tied with safety pin
on his coat, his clipped haired, large face cat
not leaving his feet, from where bending I pick
the passport up.

1997

201

AHMET GÜNTAN (1955-)

ROMEO AND ROMEO

The Hour of Sleep

Seeing me   he came from you
wanting himself, love, I was in you,
let him take from me, the wanter, what he wants

I am near you, I came near you, me,
hasn't flown yet, will go then,
you, time then, for your want.

Waited for your arrival, with you,
near, next someone someone, with me
I'll love him, he forgot it before,

Forgetting, he slept, the before, with the one there,
but he says he compares tears to me, his better self,
sleeping forget, said, hey you, the one here.

More than me you, I'll remember, I
sleep in you, me
if you want to see, come, look where I sleep.

Romeo, my Romeo's leaving me,
when you wake up, turn back, my lover, here, towards you,
as I sleep, me, on the road you meet, me, I'll meet you.

I had arrived, here, I want to find, here, again,
as I wake up be near me   you found me
only I love as much as you love me, you.

Don't lie, love invisibly, me,
there where you spent the night
search me, can you sleep, then, near me, in you.

Let's sleep, let's, one-two-three-thirty,
four-five-six-thirty, seven-eight-nine-thirty,
ten-thirty, sleep time.

Once more, once more, once more,
I want to start from scratch.

Once more, once more, once more,
what doesn't stop   stop.

Once more, once more, once more,
what runs away, follows.

Lullaby

I'm with myself, alone, for myself,
walking around, me, taking you out,
who, u-turning, takes within you, me.

I won't be, here, you,
from where you sleep, I continue, as I wake up, me,
where you forgot, I start, as I forget, you.

I won't forget, what I forgot, fooling, you,
you forgot what you did, did me,
you sleep when I wake up, in your sleep tell me, me, what you got to tell me.

What I sleep with, before I sleep, give to me,
wake up, you I feel sleepy I must go, to me,
sleep with me, see what turns up, turns to where I turn, to you.

Sleepy, you can wait for my waking up, what it will give is me,
waiting to wake up I see, you,
in sleep, waiting waiting for your waking up, in me.

Little left, to my sleep, if you feel unsleepy, follow,
you forget what you forgot, the target in sleep, me,
what I'd forgotten I didn't, I, you.

Once more, once more, once more,
I want to start from scratch.

Once more, once more, once more,
what doesn't stop   stop.

Once more, once more, once more,
what runs away, follows.

Sleep

Sleeping you depart,
forgetter of your leaving is, me
as I return from sleep, get,
you return from sleep, you.

As I return from sleep
if you return into
me, there forget
what it forgot, you.

Sleep with me, you,
in sleep you depart, from me,
in sleep I forget, I, I
depart, from you.

The sleeper departs, departer sleeps,
the mark in sleep, me,
I'll lull to sleep,
in me, what repeats itself.

Once more, once more, once more,
I want to start from scratch.

Once more, once more, once more,
what doesn't stop   stop.

Once more, once more, once more,
what runs away, follows.

Dream

Looks for a simple thing: your looking for me
I do not object to, he'll pursue his objection,
I do not look for you the way you do
me, the one I look for does exactly as I want him to, me.

Very simple, it, to me, you will show me,
as you look in your manner for me, I'll still be there,
whatever turns up, fetch and show me,
in my searching place, I'll find and return me.

Very simple, what I look for is pure, not in you, you aren't in me,
come, find me, I am asleep in you,
you were fooling me in my sleep, me
from me, come, sleep in it, you, desiring me

Very simple, it'll make me sleep, your sleep, me,
without knowing with whom I'm falling, in love with you,
didn't catch on, someone, he is looking for me
fool him, show him, again to no one

I want to return to the beginning, once more,
lie down, if you want to forget, lie down then forget
is there someone by you who knows, who can know
you're sleeping, now then forget me.

Once more, once more, once more,
I want to start from scratch.

Once more, once more, once more,
what doesn't stop   stop.

Once more, once more, once more,
what runs away, follows.

The Hour To Wake Up

Come, he said, let's carry it together, he said.
As much as I can carry, I said.
As much as you can carry, he said.

You are leaving, don't, stay here I said, he said
I said don't go far he said, he says.
am not leaving, I'm staying, I said.

Sleep makes one rest he said, I said.
Sleep erases things he says he said, I said
I listen to the bitter end, I said he said he says

He opens, I said, the door, I said,
to me I said, it's true I said.
there, I said, is visible, I said, the arriver, I said.

He's shutting it to me, he said,
I'll open it, don't you worry I said, he said.

Justice Romeo!

Justice, my Romeo!

1995

LALE MÜLDÜR (1956-)

311
series 2 (*turkish red*)*

builders of the idea of turkish red
poets dervishes and wandering lovers sitting
at a drinking table based on the
refinement of ancient times
     turkish red
child sultans
looking at the reds in Selçuki tiles crying
     turkish red
the manner of eating oysters & serving them
the entering to the salon & the use of napkins
the liveries of the servants at the table & their *from-the-right-and-the-lefts*
entering the restaurant & picking a table
athenian banquet tables and Euphrates nights
as I was thinking of these thoughts
     turkish red
thinking of an Azerbaijan girl
with her crescent and star earrings
I am building the
tie between

---

*Müldür spent several years in Belgium married to a Belgian painter. Different color titles of the poems in *The Book of Series* refer to the names of specific colors in her husband's painting box.
  Words in italic in the translations mean that the words appear in the same language (English, German or Spanish) in the originals.

the lights of the bridge
           and its shimmering
           reflections in the water
seeing the water as a necklace the bridge
   as a star-crescent body
      (*
_____ = turk

   bridge

like a bridge, departing from myself
like a Turk, red, I am crying *turkish red*

1991

series 2 (*turkish blue*)

Such winds suddenly changing directions
migrating-south cranes a weird
polka like spinning in the wind in
always such same departure and co-
ming leaves with each other
embracing yell-
ow spin-
ning wed-
ding
turkish blue
someone always waited for
now not waited for or waiting
that is getting used to returning home
and putting on the fire under the tea getting
used to everything but still crying a little
a little smiling and now YOU!
will a blue bed be also
YOURS *turkish blue*

1991

548
series 2 (*blauwviolet*)

thinking of you I always find the equation of the strait line
which passes around cape hope creating an 8 degree
angle with the polar axis, *blauwviolet.*
an eagle is migrating under two dancing butterflies.
under wet mao grass someone is *l* laying a pair of
pearl earrings. to the annals of martyrdom a *t*
tear of ice is falling. window swallows
and city swallows losing their direction
are migrating towards the north and my heart *i*
is always broken thinking of you, *blauwviolet.*
as if in a *rooom* dedicated to *youu* in my heart
you are kindling some grass thrown in one corner and
my eyes like secret bamboo chests are
bowing to their secrets. as an earthen pot's
breaking because of what it holds and protects
is illogical, I am going to a deer hunt
chasing myself or
we are going. i am saying good-bye to my kin
and we are going on a long river trip until
blauwviolet waters cover our thrones . . .

1991

WAKING TO CONSTANTINOPLE
to Sophie and Gérard

looking at Byzantium you are sleeping. but your tiredness is very deep.
your tiredness as deep as a long river.
pluck and throw out your heart. that's all. that's all. this is you.
you are hearing a sound, dark rain, an anxious sound
becomes his in the yellow moon.

and then? then you are sleeping. you are sleeping inside Byzantium. first drops
falling from votive candles are burning your eyelids. a black tramp steamer
is waiting for you in sleep. a steamer as beautiful as black death. at the edge
     of sleep.
if you wish from inside sleep cutting like a black wing you can reach
that steamer. but you don't want to do that. you now on the Golden Horn on
     the water
are stretching one arm tied to a black steamer the other
to the well lit grief of the Tower of the Maiden. you were going to be torn
into pieces if you hadn't woken up.

but this isn't the first of the Byzantium dreams with Lions.
nor the last gasp of a Byzantium of being torn and waking up.
then continue your sleep for the sake of a new Byzantium awakening with Lions
but do it a little bit higher, with a bit more composure so that
the thing sliding over the gray curves, leaping over
each other, passing by in the waters of the Tower of the Maiden, no
one can tell, is it a swan or a lion? let them think it is only a fierce wind
or a shimmer drawn by an eastern comet passing on the Bosphorous years
     ago. but knowing eyes
those who stir history up a bit will remember:
any maiden who had a flighty tongue and required protection and was shut
     in the Tower of the Maiden, suddenly in an ancient Byzantium miracle

would find

herself in the Byzantium dream with Lions. this way being protected
she was punished, and being punished in a miraculous Möbius reverse she was
protected again. legends say that that thing was one of
thousands of Constantinople girls who dance the hula hoop during the day
and at night had Byzantium dreams with Lions.
but for some others it could, it could only be one of the ancient Byzantium Lions
who remembered it was a maiden once and dreaming of a maiden continuously
in a sense strived to sustain her existence.
anyhow, it is clear that this Byzantium lion fading away in the waters of
the Tower of the Maiden
isn't the one which was put right next
to the horses erected later on in Saint Marco's Square
in Venice (horses which
also came from Byzantium). . . . As
history does not permit such pleasurable coincidences, the poet too
who bears the weight of writing's responsibility
and honor, enters the scene here, ending
the Byzantium dream with Lions, aware that the few meticulous readers
who still are unable to move from pleasure principle
to reality principle and the peanut gallery
are in danger of taking seriously these narratives
of dream. yet, truly sensible readers of Ottoman Stamboul aside, other few
innocents but Byzantine readers and the mob won't
stand their stories to be broken in the
middle, flooding the fairy tale to life, that is,
to the arenas, to the streets, will want this time to see the writer
in the Byzantium dream with Lions. And right at this point, as blues and
greens are about to tear the writer into pieces, in the strange evolution of
a Möbius twist, the writer finds herself inside the game she created. and
the Byzantium dream with Lions continues. . .

you are sleeping now. you are sleeping looking at Byzantium. your tiredness
is very deep because to see Byzantium, to be able to see it took a long time.
   on the white
papers next to you reflected from the Venetian crystals on the ceiling
   bouquets of light
are falling. your eyelids are dunked in the liquid gold
of tiredness, night strewing from their edges. to remain as something
only belonging to you, not having anything taken away from you, you want
   to join up
the emperors of long sleep. for this you left your house, came up to Pera.
   sleeping now in
Byzantium's gilded waters. you couldn't choose a better place to live this
   anonym-
ity. by you there is a table clock whose tick tock can be heard. no one in the
   streets
now. a nightoid on his motorcycle is climbing the Galata Tower. listening to
   Marianne Faithful, the Boulevard of Broken Dreams. . .

night is long, you have no name. night is as long as the name of a Chinese
   restaurant — long green black yellow river . . . next to you is a pocket
   watch. why are you so
young, why are you so without worries. a voice is heard, dark rain, Byzantium,
   which in the silver dust moonlight later ends up his. you wanted to pick the
   days you lived,
the nights, the idioms, the people, but you couldn't, instead
looking at Byzantium you are sleeping. Zeus doesn't blow behind your ear any
more. Hermes in a reverse movement of the hand is not passing a bribe.
mermaids are long dead, their corpses somewhere in the open waters of the
Tower of the Maiden are drifting . . .
their silvery scales are withered. . . . a half gone voice lingering in their ears . . .
"Panthaselia, my wounded kid sister" . . . keep on drifting . . .

you are tired now are sleeping looking towards Byzantium are dreaming
of Tadzio from Venice, all that mystical fullness you are looking for. Tadzio
   is turning back
and with his index finger is pointing to the distance. now you are
having a dream. you are too remote to see the distance between Tadzio's sign
   and the space between Leonardo's mystical index fingers. Fingers in
   Leonardo's paintings
   point to some spot in the sky.

you are sleeping now/why you forgot that science/knew it
before/was taken long long ago/was taken from
you/maybe why now/your eyes shut/don't hear it/yet still may be/
at a spot pointed by those fingers/you are sleeping/you aren't far/no one is/

you never understood that Tadzio was a silhouette, a far shadow, didn't exist,
that it only existed in proportion it was a test to put you through
a ring of fire (and that consequently you also only existed for him in the same
   connection), never understood
that lives should not be ruined because of Tadzios . . . because Tadzio is you
   . . . can only be you . . .
tomorrow is your birthday . . . tomorrow, you must wake up . . . must look for
   Tadzio in yourself . . .
must catch within yourself the naivete you left behind in your sleep . . .
Constantinople must wake up too . . . ,
realize that it is the Polis of Constantines . . . each Constantine catching the
   Polis
         (those old sunken cities)
within himself, must let Tadzio go . . . must start forgetting Istanbul once was
Constantinople . . . tomorrow is your birthday, you must wake up tomorrow.
there is a pocket watch by you. Why are you so young, why are you so
worriless.

in the white washed and byzantine room one of the ancients is saying:
"here is a delightful balance: artist and human being
                         distinct and the same
                         both have gauged the depths
                         is that life is that beauty"

you are asleep now in the white washed byzantine room, you are very
alone. one of the ancients is saying, "Don't cry."
"Tomorrow is your birthday. Tomorrow a new name will be given to you."

1991

VIRGIN MARY'S SMOKE

I.

Every angel is cruel, 13 months
spent tied by Virgin Mary's rope.
That leap moon year*
terrible i-dont-know-why angels
separated us.
On the 19th week of my melancholy,
I got to recognize you. Certain things suddenly
seemed to change, as if not dragged any more
before that rabid horse called sadness.
Then a terrible sleet went down.
Winds fearfully blew. The Star of the Southern Cross
stirred. It was week 19
of my melancholy. Every angel sees
our back and our front. beyond our power.
The leap year separated us.
Why things which will end are started, my darling,
why does a Mohammedan rose suddenly bloom
why does hail fall as big as tears?
On a black satin sheet
I am tracing a gold cross for you.
Only this way can I express your absence.

I'm opening my eyes widely
to the wind of broken glass pieces
puffed on by angels. you don't show up. Black maned brown horses

---

Leap moon year: The Islamic calendar is lunar. Every thirteen years a month is added to the
year. That is a leap moon year, a year made of thirteen months.

come to my cold room. Fallen comets
come. Angels who blinfold themselves
in black come. You don't show up.
There is no reason. No reason whatever.
In churches girls pray to ikons
for our sake. A horrible sleet coming down
outside, more horrible than the angels
pulling our rope. don't know, maybe, we committed
a terrible sin. I am wrapping around my
hermit's clothes.
13 months'll pass this way. The Star of the
Southern Cross will smile at us darkly.
I'll sing songs my tongue couldn't quite twist around.
The charm someone started
I don't know why will flow by me
for a leap moon year.
I will want to wash my hand,
maybe go back.
But I won't be able to return.
Over that black sheet with a gold cross
the leap moon year will flow.

O sole mio! O Sole Negre!

II.

St. George couldn't slay either
this unknottable love in me.
Idle, Michael
famous for not smiling
coming to my rescue

with his angels.
Silence! Soulward!
I am spending my days in silence
as if in baptism in the sacred waters of Aisasmos.
In know the pitcher will crack in April.
What what else would happen, did you think?
Angel and Satan nestling, both
leave something in one's heart.
Silence! Soulward!
Everything must be kept as if a big religious secret
nothing, no frozen smile on the lip
nor even blind Spentasios's angels
should blurt out
the secret.
No need for me to sob before the rabbi.
pray only, only pray.
Maybe tomorrow will be lucky,
everything may change.
The pearls of mourning and the Angels of Rome
will recede
Shh! Even this is too much.
Silence! Soulward! Did you ever think?

"And Adam loved God
and Eve loved Adam loving God."

III.

They'll try to eliminate us with this obvious
black plot.
They are casting cursed glances at my house,

squeezing their eyes as owls
pretending they know nothing.
Shh! Silence! Soulward!

"O my people, what have I done unto thee." *

Not expecting anyone,
as Virgin Mary, great star of the Sisterhood of Love,
was caught in her dirty towel by Gabriel, the Angel of Death,
this way, we also are caught, by our warms glances towards
each other, as though there is a dirty towel, a night gown
somewhere.

That's her, remember me, remember me,
I used to wash your feet,
your muddy, sinner's feet
Ricorditi di me, che son la Pia;
Ricorditi di me.

O my people.

IV.

> "Apricot flowers are blowing from East to West
> I tried to keep them from falling."

How fast the summer passed with flutes
a raspberry rain is coming down now
grandfather dozing inside

---

*Italicized words appear in the same language (English, Spanish) in the original.

in that wet country of raspberries
                    the elegy of the Jerusalem Virgins starting.

How fast the summer passed with rainstorms
the woman sleeping on her rug
she is a raspberry country now
an angry and fearsome song
                    starting in her heart now.

Did I want to return
did I
          to to being without you,
          to that pagan country?

To return with rock 'n roll pieces behind me
return in my coquettish decadent Venetian clothes
return to a bunch of my flirts waiting for me
CONTRA NATURA

and say, "I'm Lazarus
          of the dead
          asking forgiveness.

Forgive me among yourselves
                    for my seeing horrible things
for leaving you with violets in my hand
                    forgive me

I want to mingle with the Jerusalem virgins
in that wet country of raspberries
to give birth to a boy
                    forget you.

V.

Remember also the episode of the Virgin Mary in the book.
That day the angels had said this:
"Hi Mary, God truly picked you,
purified you and declared you
superior to all the women of the other nations of your time."
Otherwise you weren't with them
when they cast their arrow of fortune
to see who'll be the Virgin's protector.
Black plotters who were left alone with their fantasies of glass houses
said: "Hey Mary, who are you
who did something so surprising,
Hey Aaron's sister,
your dad wasn't anyone bad
your mom not a whore."
Upon this Miriam winked at Jesus.
Upon this Miriam winked at him.

Miriam, Imran's daughter, her mother Hannah!*
Top of the women in paradise!
Poor Miriam, who is constantly thinking!
When her hair was let loose in the wind, young poor Miriam!
"What could it matter," she said, "if I'd died before,
before and hadn't seen these days . . ."
She wasn't this lonesome
before.

---

*In the Eastern Orthodox tradition, Imran was Moses's father. The word "Meryem" in Turkish refers to both Miriam, Moses's and Aaron's sister, and to the Virgin Mary. Lale Müldür is playing on the different meanings of the word, hinting that the speaker also has Jewish connections. In the Islamic tradition, 'children of Imran' refers to the Jews.

"Mary, who are you then?
        Queen! Queen!"

This is the Mary episode angels were discussing.
The guilty should know
The day they'll meet the angels
there is no good news
for them.

Except for Mary and her son
all born infants
are touched by the devil
and for that children start screaming
as soon as born . . .

VI.

Melancholia!
Memorabilia! . . .

"The Angel wanted to stay a bit more . . .
but the storm which blew from Paradise
captured its wings so forcefully
that it couldn't fold them again."

The Angel of History,
face turned back,
helpless in storm,
dragged to the future . . .

Untouchable like Euridice
which arrived at a new girlhood.

When suddenly,
god holding her by the hand, eliciting with a sad scream
the words: "Looked back!"
she understood nothing, said quietly: "Who?"

VII.

Mark: the light on Mary's elders' forehead

On her elders' forehead
a password was being written: MHMD*

Theirs is a race which emerge
from each other

Mary's pearl birth.†
It's said that sometimes the oyster rises to the surface of water
and like a firmamental womb pulls rain into itself
it's said that pearl is good for melancholy
unpierced, virgin pearls . . .

---

*The consonants which make up Prophet Mohammad's name in Arabic. This poem points to the
continuity through Judaism (Mary as Miriam), Christianity and Islam (and Greek Paganism).
†Müldür is punning here. "Incil" means *The New Testament* in Turkish. "Inci" means pearl.
When she says Mary's pearl birth," she is also implying her birth in *The New Testament*.

VIII.

Miriam al Basriya
was in the service of Rabia al Adawiya
listening to the science
of the Love of God
she immediately fainted.

During one listing trance
she died of love . . .

God has housekeepers who resemble rain.
Falling in the soil they become corn, falling on the sea they become
    pearls.

IX.

the universe is composed of four elements.
whichever you choose, you're up cripple creek

A rose: burning in fire
        drying without water
        drowning without air
        freezing in marble.

X.

last light in my dream on the train I boarded as a stowaway
I was looking for sea salt. Salt and a white horse! the image of Christ!
To create salt itself, which gives taste to everything, is impossible.

I finally understood the black plot. exactly like Nerval,
I also preferred the created to the Creator.
With visions of love and death, to forget my remorse
I began hiking on meadowy spaces.
Nerval asking for forgiveness in the church before Suffering Dead Mary
dropping his ring with the names of Allah, Mohammad and Ali inscribed
     on it,
suddenly all the candles light up
and *Ave Maria* starts.
A small flower blooms on the hills of the
Himalayas.
Do not forget me, also.

XI.

a strange mystic thing
your being so familiar
is perhaps due to our having met before.

wrapped in an old fur i am stretching
now in the room / thinking of you
doors windows forms
are softening and disappearing
white cloudlets are filling the room
the moment I seem to fly
over the clouds
I am touching something odd and fearful
maybe part of an idol
                    or of a white horse which is coming alive
                    maybe an unfinished part
a horse about to be created

in a cloudy essence
in the original matter!

maybe i was passing through an angel . . .

XII.

whereever i look i was meeting the scarlet sign of sin.
the easterners westerners northerners southerners feudalists
aristocrats bourgeois laborers artists toasters
jews christians moslems. the pearl inside the oyster
is the genius which thinks at night, like my last utopia, the moslem
community. but they also separate like broken delicate pearl necklaces.
whereever i look i was meeting the scarlet sign of cruelty
i decreed the end of the world and became a cold
cold woman, a Lady d'Arbanville.
A FLOWER ABOUT TO BLOOM
WHICH SUDDENLY CLOSES
A MEDIEVAL LADY
AN APASH AT THE START OF LOVE
AND A CHASTITY BELT AT THE END
YES BUT WHAT PITY WHAT PITY
OUT OF A HOT BLOODED CHICK LIKE ME
THE WORLD CREATED A LADY D'ARBANVILLE
YES BUT WHAT PITY WHAT PITY

I'M STILL GLAD
THE QUARTZ SIGN OF MY CHASTITY ON MY FOREHEAD
SLEEPING IN MY COLD BED

OH LADY MARY, THE LADY OF LILIES

AT SNOWY MEDIEVAL NIGHTS TAKE ME TO YOUR SIDE . . .

"The world declared her mortality,
and she keeps looking back."

therefore, crying
they veiled her face . . .

A. . . I, Barnabius from Cyprus, . . . (. . .) . . . being completed
by God of the worlds worthy of prayer beads
hearing of being martyred for Soulful Jerusalem on a
Jihad . . . loyally . . .
at 48 years' (sky years) end . . .
. . . in 4 iron versions . . .

lonesome . . . is it how it is?

You will say thus to them:

"I won't live in your town long . . ."

THEN LIKE A NAME

THEY'RE ENTERING A DIMENSIONLESS SPACE

1994

THE YELLOWING
translated by Maggie Dubris

the weeping sweet baby the mint leaves swirling . . .

the kids are wearing their colors baby
oh it's only knives they're happy
oh I forgot that song
the kids are wearing their colors baby
just don't jump on every horse in town

that lone blown boat from the east
you learned long ago its name is sadface
oh the happy knives from the north
the blood and mint leaves swirling
in the hot copper sun
pull your hood down
in this bloodstorm baby this mintstorm

nothing matters to know nothing matters to you
you turn away you fall asleep
my sighs your lullaby my knife so sweet and true
you might be tiger butter tiger you might be hard as gold
so here — I'll tell you what I know
get out of this bloodstorm this mintstorm

the kids are wearing their colors baby
gone to Arizona to passion and sorrow
the men wear the bucket-of-blood there baby
black heart called — *adios, mis* little *cholos*!
see I forgot how but I made my mark

with my laughing heart with my rusty knife
cause baby you're a piss-brain if you stir it up this time

the piss-brain slides on his snakeskin baby
takes a little walk with Mister Lucky on his lips
pedal to the metal out on Route 66
the piss-brain wears beer-goggles to read with baby
has a mouthful of barfing-barfing-shoot the buffalo
in the canebrake by the lake with *Night Fever* playing low
but shit he's never old he's never old he's never old

a lone stoned boat putt-putts through the ice
rust gets in my eyes the skies go yellow
just make my tea with tears the mint leaves swirling
call it kamikaze shaken call it pollen on the rocks
its name is loves-me loves-me loves-me loves-me-not
blues strained through yellows only leaves
and sepals sepals and hair
messy with chicky-chick of *noche noche no*

in a tinkling of knives
a cloud of fireflies
love showed up crackling light cracking light
I rose sadface I got
an armful of oranges
made time stop then made it go
chitchitchatchatontheyellowdaisymat
like the sun and her shadow

well love slipped out the back way
in the blast of a horn the rain of pollen
headed west into the violets

and sepals hair
matted with the chicky-chick of
y el noche noche noche
something twined around my heart
it was just a lost tornado
folding up his wings
in this cold dark forest
in this land of yellowing
ye el noche noche noche
just look at that light
it falls like gold dust through the night

. . .

1990

HAYDAR ERGÜLEN (1956-)

CARAMEL

My burnt candy is hard. My life worse,
Forgetting that both come from the same shit
but I took, took to loving a woman, as life
scent of cinnamon, Carmen, oh, Carmela
she loved crème de menthe, but I compared
her to the steam from coffee and
she must have compared me to something
she took to the ache of love now she
is thrilled with leaving.
Love it seems preceded us and opened shop
early in the morning, recognized it
by its smell, its spices, its painful
words I took as the salt and pepper
of love, met her moods
in old accessory shops:
the Mirror Arcade, Bon Marché, the Gold Button . . .
A thousand habits, a thousand choices
clashing together,
I came across a store's stone walls, door locked,
neither my sweet words can open it nor my moody poems,
then I found it was a caramel shop.
Now, my burnt candy is hard, my life worse,
but I am aficionado, separation is worse.

Oh, my sweet caramel, caramel is sweet but not its eaters.

1997

PLACID

The words of the house are stone, walked to the balcony
the words of the house are heavy, as though unuttered
for a hundred years as though
completely out to lunch. The dead are eulogized,
the living mentioned. If we'd just looked at the placid water,
if we'd stopped this house, as if pulled off their foundation
the words of the house gushed . . .
The visitations from the boxwood, laurel, honeysuckles on the balcony
were from the first day, greens also
whose names I don't know. To those which we watered I think only yesterday
today we brought words, a sweet basil was left under my hand,
which I caressed like a cat, it filled my hand
but not the heart of the house, the house is
heartless. The insistence of the full moon was in vain,
in vain the blowing of the breeze, this is called
house storm: it awakens words, drags the house,
the rain of words bends the neck of flowers.
If the house hadn't gone mad, we could have talked of life's beauty
staring at the placid water.

the nature of the house is more inimical to life than furniture's, it seems.

1997

NİLGÜN MARMARA (1958-1987)

. . .

Love is a kilim,
plus its walls, a tiny sea.

. . .

1988

MUSTAFA ZİYALAN (1959-)

DAYS

One.
First,
first.

without anything else —
being.

Seven.
heaven.
enlightenment
in the twilight mascara
of your eyes.

Eight.
according to you, a zero tightening its belt.
according to me, two zeroes kissing.

Ten.
a stick and a hoop rolling in the nocturnal meadows.

Eleven.
Sleeping back to back.

Thirteen.
I love differently, please lie a different way.
don't wrinkle your nose — talk to me.

Fourteen.
No thirteen.
Are you dozing off or just keeping quiet?

1990

KUMKAPI, BY THE SEA

a house,
not
by the sea,
on the farthest end of the railroad,

its shuttered windows,
full of geraniums,
its iron gate open
for the cat,

but she wasn't there,
her husband a retired
railroad man,

wearing a pocket watch on a chain
a cigarette case and a lighter
in a robe,

but always addressing his wife as "my dear lady"
kids horsing around on the sofa
the calendar of the education ministry
on the wall,

but always late,
(*your aversion to remove its leaves . . .*)

who is going to drink tea with the Greek neghbor?
who is going to feed the hen with the missing leg?
who is going to mourn, for those who die before their time?

1990

THE SHAPES OF CLOUDS

between scorpion
and wind chaser*

time is a blur

air shovellers

Or this grandad
clock

has a pair of scissors

or a funny
moustache.

---

scorpion/ and wind chaser: the literal translation of the hour and minute arms of a grandfather clock in Turkish.

GRANDFATHER CLOCK

It used to play
with me

me on the carpet
and it
against the wall

OEDIPUS DE-BONED

I heard while my dad making a date with woman at the next table
a stranger across me deboning my fish

. . .

2001

241

from ISM'S

14.

wing
broken,
arms also
broken,
flying
we,
you heart
& me,
mother
flying,
i'too'm flying
ma,
homeless
endless

16.

your silence,
in
this
face,
also
is full.

18.

a touching
kin ship.

19.

kisses,
why
unending?
from where,
where seaside,
to where?

20.

the one
before
as the one
later
is yours.

24.

when
it darkens

the corpses
smile

in mass

25.

did
we
live
in
my
burial?

26.

Later,
then younger,
than me.

29.

while she smiles
the lips
of heart ache
on my mouth.

32.

The door collapsed
by the absence
of wall.

36.

pa,
of the smiling face,
always windy thoughts
behind it.

39.

erased
apple
left

its
shadow
on
the
wall.

2001

SEYHAN ERÖZÇELİK (1962-)

A dream in Istanbul of falling
a falling dream
Istanbul is falling in a dream
falling in Istanbul in a dream.

1991

DUŞTANBUL */

İSTANBUL

DÜŞ — TO FALL
      DREAM/IMAGINE

TAN — DAWN

BUL — FIND

247

from PLATONIC

I.

The evening folded
blind, plato blind
folded.
Someone writes rain
rain
writes
rain rain.
Eyes black, yours
eyes eyes
bible black.

II.

Put China! Put a pinch of chinese in your eyes,
darkest inside. "puts China
in her eyes," they'll say, "celadon chinese
inside her eyes. Ignorant of
being porcelain. Let me move you
with care; don't worry, don't crack. On your
eyebrows apply
gold standard. The clock. A loop. At ten past, sixteen,
down silk ladder,
let's.
the clock, stuck.
Ear, ring! Run
Out the loop.
Your foot slips,
the clock strikes

248

celadon cracks,
darkest inside,
tang!

1991

from COFFEE GRINDS*

"In our house lilies, roses,
magnolias, jasmines are blooming, while you are reading fortunes,
while I am watching, while I am reading fortunes,
while you are watching."

SEVEN

There, a road to outside from the cup, already visible, before lifting it up. That obvious.

O.K. To where?

A shard is peeling from you, what's unfolding on the road is it.

Two of you, sitting and talking, besides, you're reading
his fortune. Who is a smoker, sitting in front of you, he is listening. You are reading to
him, reading,
reading, so intensely that from you to him,

Coffee Grinds is made of twenty-four coffee-cup readings.

and him to you, something is shuttling, shuttling something between you two.

Three roads, the middle of which is a tributary of the road outside from the cup, you are crossing seas.

The cloud in the air is a splinter.

Like a bird with a long beautiful tail to distances, under a crescent mooned light, the crescent moon waning for the next full moon, a wide joyful road is starting out of the mouth, that is, you are coming out and leaving.

O.K., to where?

Not that fast. Tossing your hair, you're also seeing off someone, like old times precisely, with a handkerchief in your hand, a kid next to you. But like seeing off someone sailing on a boat.

Someone leaning on your breast. Who that one is isn't visible, isn't legible. He's holding the star in his hand.

251

Your fate's in that star.

Then a rooster. A new rooster, cockadoodledooing in the moonlight.
Ushering good news. A kismet, which will please you. And a cat also is letting itself be caressed.

Every coffee grind is you.

Which are endless.*

Pouring what was left on the saucer back in the cup, a new fortune.

The grinds are reforming themselves.

Whichever way I may play with the cup, I can't change your kismet.

252

---

* Like coffee grinds themselves, fate is splintered into different words,: coffee grinds, fortune, luck, kismet, rooster, dolphin, cat, fox. One can see in this language its animistic, Central Asian origins.
Fate as a unifying concept is not spelled out, but referred to obliquely in its different manifestations, an unnamed core around which the coffee grinds weave their infinite pattern.

That's the way the cookie crumbles . . .

(Ill fate, well made.)

EIGHT

A mass of coffee grinds's flying to the sky. A profound sadness is getting up,
about to get up, and leave, leaving behind its space
empty, that is, nothing to interpret
in its stead. Either for good or evil.

A portion of universe waiting to be filled, is what's left.

Something has ended, you're relieved, have gotten rid of a burden.
(What the load is, I can't tell.)

Inside the cup further back, a dolphin. The greatest of luck,
the most propitious object. Both a fish, and with lungs. Besides . . .

It'll drag you with itself, to the sea.

To the sea or the sky? If sky, is freedom, sea is mother's lap.

To the sea or sky? Various cats and roosters are also dragged with you. You're on the road
on a royal progress, together, towards somewhere. Two roosters, one cat and the fish.

The dolphin leading the way, a lucky and fortunate road.

(An event, clearly, affecting the whole family, by the way, good luck.)

That's what is beyond the emptiness. Something happened, you are freed. This is affecting a lot of people near you, along with you.

Affecting well and good.

A good reading. Wonderful.

Well, that's it.

255

NINE

You are stretching for a fish. Fish, that is kismet, watch out . . . the Holy Dolphin!

Two people obstructing you. Holding the tail of the fish, they don't let go.

Kismet isn't only fish, there's also a rooster flying over the fish. Nothing is preventing it from reaching you, but it's better if you can obtain the fish first.

Besides the rooster is a lesser kismet than the fish.

(Interpret kismet as money, luck, ease of heart, a swoon of heart, however you wish.)

You'll experience a minor distress, but it'll easily go away.

There are two roads before you, directly relating to you. Because of that you'll be forced to make a decision. And you must make it soon and fast.

Depending on it, you can reach the fish, that is, going back, if you choose one of the roads, a fish will appear before you.

(In this case, the idea of obstruction is an issue. Choosing the other road, there is neither a fish nor those holding it by its tail.)

Coffee grinds in your saucer also, exactly in the middle divide in two.

Or two opposing but equal forces, coming face to face.

Which shows how hard it will be for you to decide which road to choose.

But decide you must, which you will.

That's it, I guess.

More, please.

Wow!
Don't ask for more.

257

TEN

Your fortune has set like the Black Sea. Untrustworthy and heavy. Let's read.

To connive something against you, djinns are holding hands, hand in hand, have reached a decision about you. It's such a chaotic meeting that the whole place is a mess. Sky and earth one.

You must consider, who, what these djinns might be.

Review acquaintances, relatives, when I say relative, I'm also including your mother.

Reach a decision.

This decision is on your heart, and is above your heart.

You'll attend an important meeting.

(Here light, the Aegean light, is piercing through the cup, with things I don't see. I never figured cups occasionally could be translucent. Fortune tellers also it seems may have inauspicious days.)

In this council, be firm. They'll try
to wheedle something out of your mouth.

Do I need to tell you that your heart is fluttering? Don't hearts
flutter inside all coffee grinds?

Yes, but why is yours fluttering a bit differently?

Didn't I just mention that djinns were stomping above your head, well these djinns are
discussing this flutter.

In other words, something major going on. (The Aegean light doesn't let me see it, besides,
one's fortune is illegible over water.)

Behind the swelling heart the horizon is tracing itself. (And it is vast. Is the tracing
boundless, or the horizon, decide for yourself.)

I'll get to the point. There is a sudden danger before you.

Handle it . . . if you can.

259

No roads in the near future either.

You'll pray, did you ever imagine it? Believing that God exists in some shape, language, within the rules of a religion, you'll pray.

Prayer, and a vow.

The coffee grinds are mixed. The Black Sea has flown, and ended. This reading has ended.

(In truth more . . . things under.)

ELEVEN

Lifting the cup up, almost all the coffee grinds slid to the saucer.

This is a sign that a great distress is soon, on the verge of being over. But you must give it a push also, to extract the distress out of you.

This sadness, this huge mass of coffee grinds has left waves of traces behind itself. But These traces can't be erased. Won't be erased.

Still, you'll start anew, an easy life. Like a bird your distress is flying and you're growing light. (Besides, what's left of the coffee grinds in the cup is so easy and open, that it can't be any better . . .)

I don't see any roads anywhere.

As for the saucer, there're two cats ready to snarl at each other. You want to rescue one, or to extricate him from the fight.

And the other?

Three, or four of you are going somewhere together. Holding happily hands.

Is that it?

That's how I read fortunes.

TWELVE

Of course, this fortune is a little dry, unlooked at a long time
fortunes dry, dry and crack, like lands with no water.
Yet fortunes are fortunes. Still . . .

From the cup to the saucer, a big chunk of coffee grinds was falling.
That is, if I had opened the cup in time, read
the fortune in due time, that block'd have slid into the saucer.
Would have.

If I had opened.

I'd have read the slipping of that mass to the saucer as an easing, as a casting
out of some distress. But when fortune *freezes*,
I can't do such a reading. Because, I can't read
the fortune of the past. No one can. This way: I'm looking at *now* . . . at the *fortune*
of fortune.*

263

---

*Water is time, the mysterious catalyst in the fate of coffee grinds. What determines the fate of an arrangement, its reading? The drinker of coffee, the cadence and strength of the lips, as they sip the coffee, how far to the drains, how much liquid is left in the cup. The drinker then turns down the cup (like cutting a deck of cards). How long does the turned down cup lie fallow, the grinds trickling down along the sides of the cup. As water dries, the fortune sets; once set, they can only crumble. (*continued*)

Think also this: between the time I wrote down
and you read this fortune, the rotation of the earth completed itself
a bit more, whatever.

(Whatever which is happening, twisting and going away . . .)

You gave birth to this distress. (Giving birth!) Consequently,
it has gained an existence outside, independent from you. (The distress!) There is
no cord between you two. O.K.,
giving birth to the distress, did you eject the placenta also,
I can't tell. Distress, to continue the analogy,
is fed by the placenta, finding sustenance, gaining its existence from it.

Did you start and go on a trip? You must tell me this part
yourself. (I told you, the inside of the coffee grinds has passed,
their time has passed.) But, if I'd looked at your cup in time
there'd have been a road. Yes, three roads. One towards the hills,

264

Then the reader interprets the coffee grinds.

A coffee grind reading is a spirit echo of the world, consisting of the same four elements: earth, the coffee grinds; water, the liquid in which they move (time); wind, the voice of the reader; and fire, the urgent queries of the listener (also moon, his/her passion) which try to rush the dilatory rhythm of fortune, its telling.

this you have to climb. One, towards the sky. You have, it appears,
to fly this one. Maybe you have done so. (Did you perhaps do it in your dream?)
The third, also towards the sky. But to the lands in the sky.

(Was looking at them, the coffee grinds crumbled. Of course, this is not
odd at all. I had a *dejà vu* , but didn't mention it.)

What else didn't I mention?

I didn't mention. (I see that the coffee grinds in the saucer have moulded. You know,
mold
saves lives. Wasn't penicillin discovered that way? Wasn't it?)

The fortune of this fortune. I snagged this one . . . let it be.

265

THIRTEEN

Lifting the cup, the saucer lifted with it then fell. This act made a sound. Before being read, fortune made a sound. Is that understood?

The mass of coffee grinds in the cup is in motion. Luck, in motion. Kismet in motion.

To where?

Towards the inside of the cup. (When I say cup, you think I mean world, yours included... don't you?)

Fortune has stalled.

I'm looking. The moving mass of grinds looks like the *Nude of Maja*, reclining in bed, hands in her hair. But there is this difference: here she is mermaid. In other words: the *Mermaid Nude of Maja*. In an ether as comfortable as mother's womb, she is reclining.*

---

*Animal spirits populate the universe, cats, roosters, fish, dolphins, mountains (also infused with animal spirits), the sea, the sky, the crescent moon, all contained within the immensity of the arc of the horizon, which is also the dome of the coffee cup, which is the dome of the sky.

The coffee cup, the universe. The *fortune* of a specific arrangement, determined by a fusion of the drinker of the coffee and the reader of the grinds. Fate is a fusion of being and looking at that being; one reveals oneself by looking at others, using the universe as a mirror.

(This mermaid isn't you. But revealing of your spiritual state, both a child and a mother. Born and giving birth. That's how it is.)

A slight danger, a fish's trying to nibble pieces from this mermaid.

This danger will be averted, you won't even notice.

Wind and sea are into each other, with places beyond the sea.

Where to?

Due to the shape of the cup I guess, a horizon in the shape of a crescent moon is also in this fortune.

Everything is so clean, so peaceful.

But in the saucer, someone is carrying a gun. What it means, I couldn't make out. (That's the part of fortune which was still in motion.)

Fortune has stopped.

(Coffee grinds don't move any more.

What about kismet?)

1997

SAMİ BAYDAR (1962-)

LEAVES

I hold under shedding tears,
a thirst pit,
at thirty,
I arrange your neckties.
Please tell me what's a good time for you.

From the wood a gazelle is escaping midnight
springing it back will take
tears — warped
wood after years.

Warm bread is waylaying me nowadays
as if I hallucinate a rabbit in the bush
if I merely take a walk in the field —
either way the house guest is gone (you
were used to this place, weren't you?) —

Before leaving on the trip
checking out
the house
the windows,
the wind is
like the first stirrings of pain on the roof

first lost foreskins of living,
yet unfulfilled.

weep. weep.

1991

WATER

Water boils.
It is the cloud of the sick,

the heat rises.
this fire is
this spring.

roots park
up the tree,
home

sick.

1985

PITCHER

The late ones are taken by death,
but it takes them early, before anyone arrives
the birds flocking to the first step
rains fighting in tears are guarding us
there are spins belonging to you, in the attracting
loneliness

Like a caterpillar the rain is flowing over him
snarled s o s is sending waves to the shore
rising in the throat to the surface, death
is putting on its gloves, at the depth of words
you whispered to those swimming

I'm not sore, just spinning firecrackers in my mouth,
what's off, eye lines will true, it seems, on my part,
the broken line is vowing
revenge — waking up crying —
the letter flowing from the lip to the eye
telling its dream

On my part, I see my salvation on shoulder ends
but I can't tell what's in the pitcher because the wall of*
shoulder ends doesn't resemble the walls in the world.
If rains fighting in tears then
like a caterpillar over the pitcher

---

*I can't tell what's in the pitcher: Water in a pitcher is invisible; one can only see its contours
("shoulders," "walls"). A poem almost beyond speech. To know what is inside the pitcher, one
has to drown; the poem is made of cadences towards that state, delineating through tears
("caterpillar rain") the contours of the soul.

the man asking for help
drowns.

1987

VIRGIN RIVER

To bathe in your water
between your face and your hair
a hand must be.

Waters are alive,
madly to love, links and links
I can't tell is it rose, is it house
how sad

I can't make it heard
your loving kiss is like a mask
glued to my face
to pull them out in memories,
hair of torture

The milk lotus won't bloom in water, go figure.
that's why waiting for this moment is beautiful
as if one single sparrow left its tail flying.

1991

SEAGULLS

Boiling in the swamp, aren't they consolations
the finders of moonlight, piano and Roman bells?
consolations dying, lose their innocence
then one understands, "i lost my breath"

When your coffin opens, smile for the new friends
complain how hard it is to carry this to carry this
my Lord, during the moments of laughter
treat me nice

In the house of shadows, the sea gulls multiply, they multiply
lit up by your flashlight . . .
my eyes, wounded by these, little empty chasms open
don't watch me, darling, watch them . . .

1996

275

. . .

In the insanity of turtles
i am the owner of useless arguments
i strolled along the shore for days.

. . .

1996

A SEA BIRD

Towards the apex of the wave created on the
surface of the ocean, the bird
draws an arc, first is on the right side of this wave
its breast grazes the water
lifting, then the wave slides right
the bird reaches above the apex
and in the space relinquished by the wave
weaves to the highest point reached by the
cresting wave
hitting it on a tangent returns
belly first the bird is now entering the vault of the arc
scaling down in the left side of the wave
the wave progressing and passing this arc
draws a circle completed
by the bird's belly on the surface of the water
or adding the waveless emptiness of the moment between two waves
    joining
to the arching vault
there is always a crest left back
by a slightly sliding wave
the surface of the sea
is full of these circles of witchery
traced in the air
as a sea bird lingers on the wave
until the wave completes its circumferal motion
between two waves adds to itself
the emptying circle
of the previous wave.

1996

JACKET*

In the pocket of the jacket, a newspaper
why did they try to make them
one? Calling them lovers . . .
drawing two figures?

It's not enough to be separate
maybe the cloud doesn't believe
it, being called rain cloud,

maybe sometimes we'll see nothing
find broken needles on the floor
rice grains.

A master key'd be nice
boards will be broken
to the line traced by a ruler
another arc will be added.

Have you ever drawn an eyelid
a lovely profile in one stroke
the weight of iron cotton
a year passing, another coming

the sky emptying
the forest is in its own room
I groped in my bed
shushed,
all together unwanted . . .

Jacket: Human life is a jacket where the wearer (the soul) is not visible. A Sufi poem is a poetry of contours. Eda is the calligraphy tracing its energy filed, as the human soul breaks and heads back to God.

I prayed to those who dropped me from my crib
sat as I was told
drinking the water they were going to give me.

The cat and I
played
I detoured my dad like black bears
like a cup mowed in two
not because I knew the danger
but because, not having added sugar and
stirred it, I couldn't empty the tea on the ground.

Two love spirits will make lamp shades out of deer legs
deer into their fabrics
a moment will vanish
they'll grow timid in life.

besides, no one is eternally guilty these days
at the bifurcation they part

Y,
one sling,
yet

in my heart
one sling shot.

1996

GIGI

Gigi, the angel of invisible meetings
we did so well making angels listen to music
kids are now embarrassed, of their big ears
angels are sleeping in the meadows Gigi
bored, they are weighing bird seeds
but not selling them to birds Gigi,
I am getting by in dust and shit,
who is attempting to remind birds
that they eat seeds,
who is laboring in the meadows Gigi,
tailors for fairy tales?

I'll croak like an idiot Gigi
like an idiot hiding my love from you
I'll seal you inside a wall Gigi
you'll be invisible but people will see you
they are onto what I saw Gigi
your wish, a broken doll in the garden,
wishing me to trip and fall
don't reveal the places I've been Gigi

1991

BAPTISMAL FONT

I used to collect horse chestnuts
I knew, I rolled in meadows
in hollows and projections . . .
which stopped them.

As half of a sliced lemon
gets moldier, forming a white line
along its edge, the holding hand-in-hand
of angels.

The rain forced to settle
inside a snail grows
field angels inside.

The girl entering a dark salon
a light, lightly, is feeling its hand on your back,
phosphorescent crayons of
erotica everywhere.

That unpossessable prepossessing sleeping child, me,
is holding a flower belonging to ancient worlds
in a book.

Drawing a baseless triangle
watching the ancient flower . . .
the ancient flower is signalling a flying coersion
to the candle, capsizes
scratched by bird's feet . . .

Fearing that you might notice
the oddness of lines delienated in emptiness
i'm not turning in the direction of the sound, then,
as if asking you to focus at an odder thing,
I'm skipping over the candle.

(Chestnuts, moldy lemon, colored stones,
cooled waters, a dry leaf, a burnt match,
a few shining objects, a glowing lid,
snail shell, a burnt out candle . . .)

As you leave the child is waking:
I'm saying here I had prepared this baptismal dish
we'll write another poem, before being turns into purity.

1988

HIS WINTER FRIEND

Don't insist.
what I gave you, long afterwards,
will make it up
if you can't go through,
before.

My later love
of no return,
my love with no return
protects them
enters a religion.

Spell and religion
are my advice
as they gave it
to me. listen.

In a mysterious land
words are drinking rum
against the cold.
return the gesture.

Don't search
without a return
what you lost.
you are in a foreign country.

In the middle of summer
it's snowing,
killing those who don't see it
growing their hatred.

283

Keep quiet my darling
snowing outside
a snow visible only
without touch.

Since his girl friend
stepped out to look for cherry blossoms
this is so.

The far away tree
what could it change
keep quiet.

Before forgetting
I am drinking absinthe,
words against the cold
are drinking rum.

Since she stepped out for
cherry blossoms
this is so,
keep quiet my darling.

1995

GUILLEVİC AND THE LEOPARD'S BED

I am daydreaming as your hands caress me.
Stretching next to you, being caressed.
Leaves are falling from trees on us.
Flying birds are letting rain drops fall from trees.
At the chasm's edge the flag of loneliness is waving.
I am standing at the edge of my sleep.
On the wing of my sleep a man watching the leaves fall from me.
Among my memories you are setting your net, am waking up with the rustling
    of leaves.
Am sleeping at the chasm's edge.
A fire lit, raking together the leaves.
A shadow long asleep must still be among them, I am saying to myself.
No one expects ash to be well behaved, but it is behaving itself.
Ashes in me, I no more want their foundation of silence.
Picking a pilfered line eternity is casually placing it over my dream.
I want neither the sea nor idle comings and goings.

The flag of loneliness is covering my face, me, at the chasm's edge,
the flag at the chasm's edge bird like is whispering, longingly something to me.
I'm forgetting the night long rain, finding instead
tributaries of desire palm and date trees, crimson iguanas . . .
like the snail impressed on you in the morning, you want everything to be right,
impatiently, so much that time is diminishing like sea moss,
leaves are shedding, besides, I'm bathed,
he watching the leaves shed on me in his lair.
A person shouldn't get soiled, shouldn't get wet, shouldn't wilt, I am pretending.
It's too hard to carry an ancient void if it isn't imagined ruined.
only in your dream.

Put other arousals somewhere else.

Here, only the leopard's bed.
Before your scream only does an obstacle rise like the sun,
whereas me, I come weeping without thinking you're waiting for me.
Casting off dead weight from my wings I'm leaving the leopard's bed,
simplifying the world with tears,
from the chasm's edge, I'm yours.
The flag of loneliness is bewildered because purified by tears.
I've no intention to bewilder it, am holding to the rocks
to the rocks
                    hitting them again and again.

Am I not in a sea of tears?
I am asking for a loftier future from my ghost.
Because I'm crying they assume I wish to live,
not considering that I want to die because I soiled
the leopard's bed.
But considering it only a little.

The rain keeps pouring, my loneliness is changing, but without a hole in it.
One must return to who is left behind for a song.
Summer not fool you, things will split again.
The leaves which shed during sleep, in our waking'll be on their branches.
the leaves which stayed on the branches, in our waking'll shed.
Summer not fool you, things will split again.
an illusion is lifting from the ground all its arms.

1990

286

HERE IT'S COMING

nothing can make us roll down the wall
neither our being kids
nor navy suits
not even our curly hair
if one must talk of an equation.

As for our shadow, as if lost in the wall
with the candle expired in your lantern
one night after feeding the kids
and putting them to sleep
opening the door, if,
standing before us,
basket on your back, with two signs on your chest
which today I would kid you about,
that was not the shadow.

A rose, if you saw a pillow before you,
a sheep, a sheep if you lay down on a grave stone.

The ambassador of our belly, the rose
we are saluting it with a hand
here it comes
we see those kneeling and saluting
kneeling and saluting.

1990

287

In my bed a wave covers me
those who draw near, at each others' skirts
try to pull each others' fate.

When my husband arrived
naked dead men on the floor,
he saw a sea of disaster
staring at me — how far how far he sleeps
in his bed.

I let myself go, gently
slipping into the water
in the land of water they dry my feet that day
I remember I have a family
someone considers himself my equal

1991

NO ONE HOME*

When my wife cried
my servants told her to keep quiet
as I, while they kiss her hand,
see it in the mirror.

They embraced my wife, daughter,
making them drink herbs, I saw it in the mirror,
she sleeping, they worship her
by her bed.

Together,
when I turn my back, I don't see what they are doing.

Before my wife my servant
puts his forehead to the ground, from his back
the top of a creature is emerging
who listens to my wife like a child.

That's what they say, I know my wife
is pleading with me on the floor, but I see
her climbing someone in the mirror
sadly I love her.

My love lifts the weights from her body
and she, growing light,

---

*The mirror is a central symbol in Sufism, the site where God, the human mind and nature can see themselves in each other's reflection. In the phenomenal world, such a state — to see oneself only as a reflection — borders on pathology. In this poem schizophrenia and spirituality join. 'No one home,' because the speaker experiences everything as seeing in a mirror, as 'it'; 'no one home,' also because the human soul is invisible, apprehended only through reflections.

can approach me
as the servant sees the blood on the floor
I see her crying in the mirror.

The servant is climbing down the stairs in the mirror
I see a postman arriving
the servant says there is no one home.

1991

küçük İSKENDER (1964-)

"Turks often fuck to keep busy." —küçük İskender

from SOULJAM

his soul was raki.
he drank the shit without water.
when i die he said
i want no white shrouds.*
    —küçük İskender, from *cangüncem*

"the Mare Tenebrarum, an ocean well described by the Nubian geographer, Ptolemy Hephestion, but little frequented in modern days unless by the Transcendentalists and some other divers for crochets."
    —Edgar Allan Poe, from *Eureka*

violence: the foreign tongue of the body
    —küçük İskender, from *cangüncem*

---

*Raki can be drunk straight with a cold glass of water chaser. Or it can be laced with water in the glass to cool its fire. Mixed with water raki turns milky white and loses its licorice odor.

one

wounded electricity complements the body,
whispers to it of the innocence of chimeras,
cinema refracts a threat, at the growing heart,
everyone pulls the boy into four winds,
puts a cock in his mouth,
the boy will mature, by his mouth. the bandit grows

two

virus: *valid* declared — validates the *main stream.*
        the boy leans over the cat, tells
        the relevant. the geriatric gas positions itself
        in a suitable lung, who would be in charge
        of the building?
mystery: *lays anchor in the capillaries. each time mother nature shoots up,*
metal is happy. action is
after this.
"condom is an insult, an *insult,*"
night begins,

the rhesus monkey having turned human on an impulse

three

jim morrison is sherlock holmes. dr. watson
pulls down his *calvin kleins.* violence, at bottom,
is a crack of yearning

four

the *great white* crosses and joins the captain's
log.
noticing its own sound,
the sea gull panics,
tilts one wing in,
the weak worm
of *ionized penitence*
in its beak,

makes *it*
ice cream, the finicky
gull   hold the sugar
cone.
boy!
"condom an *insult?*"
ocean
sunset.

five

the darkling cat too needs the boy. his family locks
the pantry.

infiltration of communication by
mechanical insulation.

reconnection prowls around
defensive techniques.

six

contra slow time

eight

your face the desert shower of necessary love,
subject to rough trade, to deposits of excess *dn*as
long held   in the mirage air

my joseph's fatal *faetal* seven year release of husbanding silo
leaning on the coat of multi colors

and *and* your

ten

beauty spot?
"don't leave,
me."

then someone shows up, no voice is disrupted. my arab *shimmer*s.
from the heat of dirty august one ascends the throne
of replete September

railroads *railroads* of sound

twelve

crystals whose majority is guerillas,
full of refractions, whilst
crowds are inclinations of the like. my bequeathal
to the future as a strain
of light.

thirteen

as a scientist in god forsaken solitude in the genesis of light
awaiting   you awaited lure of transparent insanity!
I am anteing up my concentration. my *suicide*
is provided for.
my sailing bags packed expertly

fourteen

guerilla majority of crystals,
with inherent fragility, *unite*!

my misfitness even
is light

mist even   light. *feather*
and sun

the seagull reneges *re* realizing it has a voice weaves *re* repents

On a skin
of sea crumbs

my mind
sores

On a skin
white as cream

by cock's
havoc
violated
in a hammock

Dream
and mid scream
and mid stream

sixteen

*am am, an ice vermin, so human goose the ice block on which i crawl
is.*

seventeen

that someone's trying to kill me
is *inlaying* my mind, as if we'd
swapped secrets
making a night of it *many, many* nights
of drowse and bruise

eighteen

in solitude, me, full of hard ons ons and ons

nineteen

horse with a broken leg in my heart
who'll shoot you?

how many whispered words mopped up by my fingers wandering on your
lips, words i couldn't catch

twenty

which lover, whose night is immortal
an immortal stagger shoulders the night.

dies at once, if i have a brother.
burns a flower, whose burning immemorial.

twenty-one

in re philosophia: a kid defines night
as an *étude* of comprehending life with his
tiny cock,

like color blindness in smell blindness
experiencing carnation as a rose,

and me, experiencing carnation in a rose.

twenty-two

in re via dolorosa: "this sadness above me,
when will it stop brooding?"

twenty-three

"ikons broken around crystal sperms are unstealable substances
adorning the ruby entered from the mouth,
the road wide open."

vita dolorosa:
"you leave or you get lost or get lost, once your voice is broken."

twenty-four

	Narcissus
"i carry a zoo in me."	takes
our love: a glass castle.	narcotics
	in —
	a —
no tangible instant,	glass —
your eyelashes will accumulate	of
	water.

twenty-seven

i bumped into them carrying confetti.
perhaps they were a bit too willing, i a bit too out of line.

twenty-nine

scanning the irradiation of my puckered fire.
on the wagon,
two night cabs heard on the low road,
the dream in which i saw my grandma
burn her koran, I interpret it as
my sexual freedom, the serenity and inner peace of not learning
one single prayer which I can recite by heart
dying. as I carry this bliss to the face of the youngster I dance with
on the dance floor and from there to the shredded documents
of a long forgotten cult   the subversive inquiry into which faetal fate,
which toxic sexual authority will it not be all the skepticism of my
soul, which I probe into the erogenous zones
of prudence and silence?
according to some *it may be a reprehensible search for love
by the planet earth.* of my poems
and of my not yet shot movies, the hot anti-matter

thirty

my identity is the befouling of what is
knowable, and the downward velocity
of becoming young.

thirty-two

love, of a not yet visible asia, is
the barely sensible skin of plants.

grandma, entered the toilet and before taking a leak seven cups, and after
five cups, she emptied on the hole.

thirty-three

s p i n i t u a l   w o r d s   s p u n n i n g   i n   b o d i l e s s   l i g h t
l i g h t l y ,   w i s h f u l l y   w h i s t f u l l y ?   w h i s p f u l l y —
w h i m f u l l y , — w h i p f u l l y   w h a m f u l l y —?   w h e r e f u l l y
w o m b f u l l y   w h i c h f u l l y   w h o r l f u l l y ,   e t c .

thirty-four

the furthest a heart scared of nightmares
may reach/*nirvana*/ is circumscribed
by the web of capillary in one's body but a system
of circulation ivying
the universe with *curiosity*
and longing,
wouldn't it
be a big step towards *negating* the deviation
inherent in the deficiencies and deflations of choosing among
food or lovers since the vitality of
science and discovery illuminated
in *pure* orgasm
only?

thirty-five

from my fractured copious heart,
to isolate the bleeding love is ever impossible . . .

mass as flesh is the implosion of energy

thirty-six

which *love fuck* has a ballistic report, but this arthritis at the joint of hope
with my soul, when when did it begin.

thirty-seven

ignorant spaces

thirty-eight

the difference between knowing that what is merely visible is woven
into what is longed for, and spelling out
that what is merely accepted is in conflict with what is rumored
about

thirty-nine

daylight, lay fallow the faces whose cracked smiles are
sucked

forty

. . . nocturnal faultlines in the bodies
of boys who approached the high tension wires of his
rough and billowing heart (that yearned for deviance),
one *withholds* from the consummation of this love,
in the radiant negativity of meshing support

forty-one

          over extending,
over exploring of myself. away from faith but very near
dissolution, a sentence, whose subject
is neurosis, whose sentence is dying, whose teleology,
mist

forty-three

my restlessness, the stabilizing fulcrum of my repose.
after pulling all nighters our peeled off hearts still
will return giddy

forty-four

flame of disinfectant in my nose, the m.o.
of grimy *per/hour* hot-
els, reality
sandwich, for
bodies in charred

sheets, slipping
a twist of half
used crack
joint into
my breast
pocket and inhaling
the responsibility of a flailing
candle light's
winded breathing   an expansion
as gas into the city,
let others still amuse themselves
with social struggle's delusional reliance on
literary struggle: i'll let no student waste me
with my deltas,
i'm it

forty-five

even if the whole house moves, a few curtains and laces
must linger, till the axis is broken
snapping into the nocturnal white noise consciousness of memory's
all . . .

forty-six
a blur of moans.

let my heart beat like a rose
running fast from the scene

forty-seven

Chrysler in a sudden
act
of a musical rudderless
shudder
sinking through

the darker hued water —
black and white
inkar
t —
(*murder
calligrams*),

carrying janet leigh's body
in the trunk

body/trunk, *psychotic*

you are carrying the body in the body/ the definition
of obsession.

forty-eight

the veiled, the one differentiated from the others, whose being kissed sets
off sirens, what is his fate?
tutorial inspires erotic capture.
whispers of bravo breathe on and brush the innocent heart.
the novice's merit badge nicks blood most often.

worm burrowing   into island pantry

forty-nine

i realize. some of us never spawned street names.

i realize. some of us never spawned nick names.

fifty

the blue of the dome disappeared

tonight the path of my angels will track
through a blind
alley.

(backed up eyelashes thwart
the unfolding of the door)

fifty-three

rain, brain. awesome harmony, a giant tumor
of knee jerk reactions. to *insinuate* into this tumor:
to be cross-examined by a bureaucracy

fifty-four

my soul the bribe given my body

fifty-five

seeing birds passing over you
if i could break their wings

is there any
lover of whose *hands hands only* statues are made,
oh, thine incorporeal hands!

fifty-six

mine gaseous hands.

fifty-seven

no other state, our doomed authority.

frost on your smoky face

fifty-eight

but in our room of the toys, dreams are shaking off
anxiously their dust.

sixty

being small boned   i could barely stand a kiss.

how the use of perception's least
common denominator, which we may call linear logic,
would in what field, in which application
gain supporters for us, and how the con
of searching for consensus in the aesthetic field
and
splitting intelligence and use
from creativity, would have a historically
utilitarian function?

sixty-one

useless!
god is useless.
i'm god

i am relieved (a fear protects myself from me),
but why do they cover corpses in snow white sheets
and the rest don themselves,
with reluctance or cruelty, in black?

sixty-four

my eyes, shadowing the wake of a ship of ghosts.
my hand, pal, hold me by the hand!

do morticians have pampered hands,
how far do their bodies bend?
dragonflies flittering on the edge of the desert.

sixty-five

life probed me. my heart lets go. "gotch ya!" my heart won't notice.

death, the *ultimate mother* fucker   i *cherish* vamping poems.

sixty-six

the humor of selling my ex-lovers' mementos to shrift shops, and their
memories to
antiquarians.
funny but sickening.
night, the piano is playing. scarletissimo.

sixty-seven

i will hate the spider crawl-
ing on me. on me, i can't kill it

sixty-eight

carnation crack in ice.

sixty-nine

what if summer's thaw started at this critical juncture?

seventy

oh, left left your divine body like a broken sculpture
in my hands!

violence is the foreign tongue of the body
fragmentary improvisations of yearning

seventy-one

verses of adventure:
which color is blowing the dancing young man,
feet and body naked,
i can not tell.

seventy-two

could you understand, the curse of a course, to be read only by a compass?

seventy-three

spring wrote me no letters of utopias, winter did.

seventy-four

your loveliness is *where*
is missing,

where is *missing*
is the air!

seventy-five

post *naked lunch*
panislamic
femininity

seventy-six

penelope's explosive reweaving
mystic riffs of absence

seventy-seven

my soul is a jelly fish, without a womb

light descends in the gutted out space of the dome.

six hundred thirty-three

don't laugh. the moment you do i'll recall the other times
you didn't.

you don't sell your body, only rent it. you whore,
you still own it, only the right to inhabit it
is given to me. a whore, sleeping with someone,
quits his body, is asked to leave it and leave the keys behind. and since a body
       without a soul
is called a corpse, no difference between entering
any old room in a whore house & fuck someone there & fucking any old corpse
       in a graveyard, my darling, obsessions of necrophilia *both.*

except for my own life, except for my own life.

four hundred and ninety-eight

I'll Have No Sons.

I'll Have No car.

I'll Have No 'Lotta Money.'

I'll Never Make Love In The Straight Way.

I'll Own No Gun With The Pearl Inlay Handle.

I'll Have No 'Literary Partner.'

I'll Win Neither The Nobel Prize Nor The Oscar.

I'll Never Be A Worthy Citizen.

I'll Never Learn A Foreign Language Through and Through.

I Won't Go Insane.

Not Having A University Diploma I'll Never Become The President. It's Really Demeaning.

1996

DİDEM MADAK (1970-)

SIR, I WANT TO WRITE POEMS
WITH FLOWERS

Sir, you get angry that I write poems with flowers,
you don't know. I hide my scattered body
behind flower curtains.
I sit in the dark, not turn on the lights.
The wound clock is ringing, ringing until unsprung.
I recall an aching love.
This is the unnecessary sheen of a knife.
I'm the illegal rain kept for years in the clouds.
Once it rains, it'll cost you.
Sir, I'm a basement girl
whose only boss is loneliness
For now I'm solid like plastic vases
but I'm worried. In a while
in your twelve E shoes you'll step
on kids in the garden.
This is not nice, sir.

"Day is night" I'm saying,
casting bread crumbs to birds.
They'll eat glass shards
in my dream, in a bowl of water,

in technicolor lego blocks.
I'm trying to tell you, you won't listen,
no, I don't think
I can wait till the morning.
One should tell one's dream immediately.

My soul was 14, sir,
it got older in the cold of a marble table.
Protsthetic legs were attached to my soul, delicate and white.
I walked in the city squeaking.
They even whistled at the prosthetic legs.
Meanwhile, an unarmed force in me
made of flowers was besieged,
on the screen *the rustling of organza* was playing.
I tried to slip away, couldn't.
Due to that, sir, writing flower poems
from the angle of my soul I find useful.
Whatever, I remember
all the movies I see.
taking shelter in the endless night of movies.
At *Sophie's Choice* I cried a lot.
If they make a movie called *kissing tetras*
I'll cry there too.
Does one forget the spinning wheel inside,
besides, I'm used to remembering.
"I'm a magpie, sir."

Sir, there are no more armadas
or sailboats.
I'll burn a large quantity of paper.
A cormorant dove into water,

lost for a while,

even if it reemerges, having swallowed the whole world,

death isn't too large a word, sir.

I know I smell bitter like chrysanthemums.

But do you know the loveliness

of a lonesome love which makes scrambled eggs with sausages

at the stove and eats it?

A rose will tell a rose, if I see it,

but I'm lying

roses aren't much for talking these days, sir.

1996

ESSAYS

In 1995, I wrote an essay entitled "A Godless Sufism: Ideas on Twentieth-Century Turkish Poetry" for No. 14 Fall issue of *Talisman* magazine. The essay focused on the poetry of the 1960's and 1970's, the movement called the *Second New*. In the last part of the essay I inquired where Turkish poetry could go from there, suggesting that Turkish poetry was in a state of crisis needing a new language for the changed circumstances of Istanbul. In 1995 Turkish poetry was in the process of going through one of its most imaginative stages, which covers a significant portions of the poems in this anthology. I was aware of none of it.

I still believe in the ideas on the *Second New* and Turkish poetry expressed in "A Godless Sufism"; but, in retrospect, it has two serious shortcomings. Discussing the origins of Turkish poetry, it overlooks the crucial place of Ahmet Haşim and Yahya Kemal Beyatlı, particularly of the former, focusing more on Nazım Hikmet and Orhan Veli. Second, it is unaware of the best poetry written during the writing of the essay.

In this section of texts, I have decided to leave "A Godless Sufism" completely intact, preceding it by a essay on Haşim and Beyatlı. The Sufism essay has an integrity of its own, and trimming its views with the hindsight of time would be contrary to the spirit of this anthology. The rest of the essays are on the poetry of the 1990's. The first group focuses on three poems, *Waking to Constantinople, souljam* and *Romeo and Romeo*, which I think, particularly *souljam*, force a new way of looking at what a poem is, at the concept of Istanbul and represent a culmination of forces in Turkish poetry.

The rest of the essays are on or around the poetry of 1990's in general. *Eda*, the central idea in this anthology, was first suggested to me by the Turkish poet Mustafa Ziyalan though the changes the concept underwent in this anthology make it very different from what he meant or may believe in. I felt it important that Ziyalan state his idea in its original form. The next essay, "The Sights and Colors of Turkey," is about the importance of seeing and colors in the Turkish consciousness.

The last two texts are both by women. The poetry of the 1990's is about synthesis, either historical synthesis between the Byzantine and Islamic past of the city or geographic and conceptual syntheses between the East and the West. Zeynep Sayın's essay, "Pornography of the Image," explores the similarities between Byzantine icons and Anatolian script-pictures. Its last paragraph culminates with the observation that both the icons and script-pictures require a constant movement of the eye in their viewing. Constant movement is the defining feature of the poetry of the 1990's.

The last text, "Are Turks Really . . . Dangerous?" is an interview about a novel, *Byzansiyya*, which the poet Lale Müldür never wrote. The interview is full of a sense of the historical importance of the city, what Müldür calls "Byzansiyyan" megalomania, a sense that Istanbul is a historical and spiritual nexus and what it says or does is important beyond its borders. This sense permeates the poets of the 1990's and is also the point of view of this anthology about Turkish poetry in the twentieth century.

AHMET HAŞİM AND YAHYA KEMAL BEYATLI : Arguments on the Origins of Turkish Poetry

Ahmet Haşim's poetry is like a voice one hears and forgets. "That Space" ("O Belde"), the chronologically earliest poem in this anthology, is written in two languages. Its main thrust is conversational Turkish, but constantly the poem is cut with phrases or poetry fragments from Arabic or Persian, as if the language he is using is not enough (he doesn't know it enough) and he has to extend outside to be complete. Ahmet Haşim's poem captures the original gesture of taking flight, the delicate, almost feminine, melancholy yearning gesture — in his case a profound awkwardness — which is an essential vein in twentieth-century Turkish poetry:

Out of the sea
this thin air blowing, let it play with your hair
if you knew
one who, with the pain of yearning, looked at the setting east,
you too, with those eyes, that sadness are beautiful!

What one remembers reading Ahmet Haşim is the birth (or rather the re-birth) of a language, originating in Asia, not used in written form since the sixteenth century. It opens a space made of new memories.

"That Space" is often published in Turkey side by side with a translation of it into "straight" Turkish. In that way, translation (in its case the Persian fragments the poet is hearing) is of the poem's essence. It represents that odd,

319

Ur space that translations try to enter and re-enter.

Other meanings of the title of the poem in Turkish:

O Belde: That Space
O Belde: In that waist
O Belde: In that semen.

∾   ∾

It is common to try to define Turkish poetry in European terms, for instance, attaching symbolism to Haşim's name. Only two foreign poets directly relate to this poetry, both from the sixteenth century. The first is the Persian Sufi poet Hafız and the other the Turkish Azeri poet Fuzulî. The references to wine glasses, roses and nightingale in Ahmet Haşim derive from Hafız; But Hafız's chiseled, elliptical, serial poetry is replaced by a sinuous, almost visual line.

The Azerbaijan area was under Persian influence in the sixteenth century. Though full of Persian words, the cadences, the syntax of Fuzulî's language is agglutidunal, spoken Turkish. As a poet writing in Turkish, the only Turkish poet Haşim can refer to is Fuzulî, no other written literature existing four hundred years in between. In fact, Fuzulî's Turkish, full of Persian words, is reminiscent of "That Space" ; but the cuts in Haşim's poem are much more drastic, only crossed by the arcing impulse of the thought. In Fuzulî, the Turkish and Persian elements are more seamless, elements of the language used by a Turkish poet.

Iraq is another connection between the two poets. Haşim was born in 1885 in Baghdad, at that time a province of the Ottoman Empire. His first language may not have been Turkish, but Arabic; he was sent to Istanbul for his education when he was twelve. Iraq's conquest by the Ottomans occurred in 1534. Fuzulî is known to have spent most of his life in Iraq, either in Baghdad or the city of Kerbela. For Fuzulî to have chosen to write his major work in Azeri Turkish, an eastern Anatolian dialect not much used for literature, is a mystery. Both poets seem to have grasped a language in conflict with the givens of their environment. That way, they are both, in Gilles Deleuze's sense, "minor poets."

Kerbela, one of two cities Fuzulî is associated with, is where the Shiite Islam was born, the sect with which Sufism is associated. Sufism is the third connection between Haşim and Fuzulî.

Fuzulî's major Turkish poem is the narrative *Leila and Majnun.* "Majnun" means "wanderer, lost, poor, crazy, a poet." The poem represents in narrative form the Sufi *arc of ascent,* the transformation from physical loss to union with God. Majnun falls in love with Leila, who comes from a prominent family. Her family refuses him. He goes mad (becomes a poet, speaks to animals) and wanders in the countryside. People take pity on him and convince Leila's father to give her to Majnun. When she is brought before him, Majnun says, "You are not Leila," so transformed was he/she from the physical person at the beginning.

"Leila" means "night" in Arabic. When the physical love for Leila disappears, her "true" identity emerges, "night." In Turkish poetry "night" is an image of extreme beauty, spirituality and fulfillment.

Leila and Majnun is a key reference for Haşim. While the references to roses, wine glasses and nightingales derive from Persian, the story of Leila and Majnun is Turkish, chosen by Fuzulî from "obscurity"; no major Persian poet uses it. It points to the peculiar quality of Turkish Sufism, its focus on suffering and disintegration of the self. Haşim's second book, *Wine Glass (Piyale,* 1926), is a series of lyrics dealing with transformations, flame-like dissolutions, through love and suffering. This theme runs like a river through twentieth-century Turkish poetry.

ॐ ॐ

What Is Yahya Kemal asking us to "see"?

The garden still plethora, with your sweetest voice
If one day you long back oh for a station of that summer

Look at the nodding water of the harbor, you'll see,
That past night lying in its depth
                    —from "That Summer"

What Beyatlı is asking the reader is to transfer the language of desire into a seeing woven into the language of Istanbul; in other words, he is establishing one of the foundations of *eda*. Time ends its split between past and present and becomes a flow, a continuum.

A GODLESS SUFISM:
Ideas on the Twentieth-Century Turkish Poetry

I. The Boat in the Water

Starting with an image of lost sailors pulling a row boat: they think the waves around themselves are made by their oars, unaware of the deeper currents, swells which are really determining their course in the ocean. The position of many Western poets, particularly in the United States, is analogous. Turkish Poetry from the late 1920's to the early 1970's, a period of about forty-five years of radical poetic activity and great achievement, is one of these gigantic forces basically invisible to the yachtsmen world anthologists in the West.

The period in question has, in fact, two stages. The first, approximately from 1929 to 1950, involves one poet, Nazım Hikmet, and a poetic movement *Garip* (*Strange*) of which the central poet is Orhan Veli Kanik. 1929 is the date of publication of Nazım Hikmet's first book, *835 Lines*, and 1950 of Orhan Veli's death. Nazım Hikmet is well represented in Randy Blasing and Mutlu Konuk's joint translations published by Persea Books in the United States: *The Epic of Sheik Bedrettin and Other Poems* (1977), *Human Landscapes* (1982) and *Selected Poetry* (1986). A selection from Orhan Veli's poetry, *I am Listening to Istanbul*, now out of print, was published in Talât Sait Halman's translations by Corinth Books in 1971. Another selection, *I, Orhan Veli*, was published in my translations by Hanging Loose Press in 1989.

Though not the focus of the present selection, a few crucial points need to be made about this period. Following the establishment of the Turkish Republic and its founder Kemal Atatürk's linguistic reforms, this poetic movement involves wresting the Turkish language and poetry from the ubiquitous presence of Persian and Arabic, two dominant Islamic languages. The result of this struggle is lightning fast and unalterable.* The language of a Nazım Hikmet poem in 1929, for example, is almost as different from the language of a turn of the century reformist poet like Tevfik Fikret as Anglo-Saxon is from modern English. (The introduction to *I, Orhan Veli* has a more detailed description of this transformation from Ottoman to modern Turkish and literature.)

The little discussed aspect of this radical transformation is its Sufi connection. Trying to establish their literary identity, Turkish poets turn to their centuries old folk poetry, particularly to the *Ilahis* (divine poems) of Yunus Emre (thirteenth century), Eşrefoğlu (fifteenth century) and Pir Sultan Abdal (sixteenth century). The divinity in this poetry is in essence Sufi. Sufism, with pre-Islamic, central Asian origins, has several characteristics. Its God is pantheistic in contrast to the orthodox Sunni branch of the Islam, whose concept of God is legalistic, based on the Kur'an. In Sufism the language of God is often intermingled, fused with the language of sex — here, more than anywhere else, one can see its Pagan, *Shaman*, source. Also, Sufism's is a sexuality where pleasure is unified with pain, hurting with being hurt, power with weakness, loss of self with finding God, a pull towards God with a pull towards sex, etc. It is also tacitly a homosexual eroticism (Turkish has no gender distinctions). In its mystical language, Sufism pulls out the officially suppressed, heretical, subversive, anti-authoritarian tendencies of the Islam (see Peter Lamborn Wilson's *Sacred Drift: Essays on the Margins of Islam* [City Lights Book, 1993]). Sufism can be an insurrectional language. An *Ilahi* by Pir

---

*Two poets preceding Nazim Hikmet by a generation, Yahya Kemal Beyatlı and Ahmet Haşim, contributed also to the transformation of Turkish.

Sultan, for instance, calling for self-sacrifice in the service of God is a coded call to rise against the Sultan.*

Sufism is a suggestive, shadowy, ambiguous, wide-ranging language of contradictory and subversive impulses. Turning to the folk tradition to establish their identity, Turkish poets bring this language of Sufism to the twentieth century; an Asian sensibility, partly submerged under the orthodoxies of the official Islam, reemerges. Crucial: this reemergence occurs in Turkish, a language radically different from literary Arabic and Persian, not to mention most Western European languages.

Sufism and Turkish are Asian in origin. The structure of Turkish reveals their common sensibility. Two principles define sound and speech patterns in Turkish, which is a declined language. Vowel harmony is the first. Vowels are divided as open or close, for instance, "a" (as in *a*rmy) as opposed to "e" (as in *e*nemy), etc. A word with a first open vowel must continue with open ones, including the declensions, and vice versa. Turkish has no distinction between long and short syllables†; that is to say, individual words in Turkish have almost no rhythmical value. Rhythm in Turkish is syntactical, in its cadences. Due to its declined nature, Turkish has a infinitely flexible word order. Shades of meaning and emphases are created by placing phrases in different parts of a sentence. This placing is also a cadence because an abstract word order haunts these variations. There is an intimate connection between rhythm and meaning in Turkish. Added to this also is the fact very often pronouns are done away with, gender distinctions don't exist and the meaning of a word depends on its position in a sentence; the sense of a particularly long sentence in Turkish must be grasped intuitively, globally. This global intimacy and the ambiguities of Sufism couple in the *Ilahi* form of the Turkish folk poetry and reemerge in the twentieth century Turkish poetry.

---

*An example of an insurrectionary poem coded in the language of Sufism is in my introduction to *I, Orhan Veli* (New York: Hanging Loose Press, 1989).
†The Turkish alphabet being completely phonetic, one letter to one sound, vowel and syllable are interchangeable.

There is in the present an intense interest in Sufism in the West, particularly in the United States. A number of translators have turned to the Selçuk poet, Mevlana Jalaloddin Rumi, a Turk who wrote in Persian. Though he is a very great poet, the choice is unfortunate. Rumi's images of "universe," "drink," "dance," "whirling dervishes," etc., feed into the sense of the East (partly deriving from Fitzgerald's *The Rubaiyat*) already existing in the West. Hooking on these already familiar images, translators miss the drastic changes English needs to assimilate the Sufi world sense and language. Peter Lamborn Wilson is one translator who is aware of this need, in addition to the heretical nature of Sufism.* The pre-Islamic, central Asian side of Sufism is clear in Turkish folk poetry,especially, in the *Ilahi*. I would focus on one of its supreme practitioners, the sixteenth century poet Pir Sultan Abdal, who was hanged for rebelling against the Sultan. In no poem I know does love turn to hurt, life to death, obeisance to God to obeisance to sex, pursuit of sex to pursuit of righteousness in more lightning speed than in the following majestic *Ilahi*. The translation is my own:

The rough man entered the lover's garden
It is woods now, my beautiful one, it is woods,
Gathering roses, he has broken their stems
They are dry now, my beautiful one, they are dry

In this square our hide is stretched
Blessed be, we saw our friend off to God
One day, too, black dust must cover us
We will rot, my beautiful one, we will rot

He himself reads and He also writes
God's holy hand has closed her crescent eyebrows

---

*In his *The Drunken Universe: An Anthology of Persian Sufi Poetry* (Phanes Press, 1988) Peter Lamborn Wilson avoids the *Rubaiyat* trap by using colloquialisms.

Your peers are wandering in Paradise
They are free, my beautiful one, they are free

Whatever religion you are, I'll worship it too
I will be torn off with you even the Day of Judgment
Bend for once, let me kiss you on your white neck
Just stay there for a moment, my beautiful one, just stay there

I'm Pir Sultan Abdal, I start from the root
I eat the kernel and throw out the evil weed
And weave from a thousand flowers to one hive honey
I am an honest bee, my beautiful one, an honest bee.

Trying to break down the molds of Ottoman court poetry, Nazım Hikmet first turned to Mayakovsky's futurist rhythms and irregular lines; but, soon, the repetitive, intimate, majestic music of the *Ilahi* replaces them. The poetry of Orhan Veli, a different kind of poet, is filled with a humorous, carousing vernacular; but, under it, one hears the repetitions of the same melancholy music, with intimations of death, which gives the seemingly most throw away lines depth. This elusive but essential quality which unites them is *Eda*.

II. 1950-1975

The *Second New*, in contrast to the previous *Garip*, is the prominent movement in the third quarter of the twentieth century in Turkish poetry. There is one major poet outside it, Ahmet Arif, whose *I Wore Down My Chain Longing For You* (1969) weaves its poetry out of the Southeast Anatolian landscape and the Kurds living there. Others may refuse to be considered part of the movement; but I do not think their work would have been possible without the contributions of the *Second New* poets, specifically Cemal Süreya and later Ece

Ayhan. I believe two ideas underlie the *Second New*.* The first is *eda*, a concept to which I was first introduced by the Turkish poet Mustafa Ziyalan.

a) Eda: the Poetics of Sufism

Eda is a term derived from folk poetry, which roughly means tone, sound, style. Every poem must have its own *eda*. In folk poetry, *eda* is a term also applied to women. A woman with *eda* (*edalı*) is one whose *totality* has allure. That is to say, *eda* as a poetic idea suggests an allure which is not concentrated on a single object, but is global, diffused in the body of the whole poem.

The *Second New* can be seen as an extended, experimental exploration of the possibilities of *eda*. A polarity underlies *eda* in the *Second New*. *Eda* can be simple and clear; its underlying source, then, is often the repetitive melody of the *Ilahi* (or its secular version *koşma*). But, in the *Second New*, *eda* is more often complex, obsessively dense, decorative in its melody. The *Second New* poets exploit the flexibility, ambiguity, rhythmic elaborations of the Turkish syntax. Nevertheless, it is crucial to understand the following about *eda*: even at its most elaborate or opaque, the physical and emotional impact of a poem, the cadences of its *eda*, are always transparently clear. This global directness is at the heart of the originality of this poetry.

I mentioned that *eda* has an erotic dimension, describing the total allure of a woman. The exploration of *eda* in the *Second New* is unified with an exploration, and trespassing, of sexual possibilities, into taboos. The obsessive theme of the *Second New* poetry is erotic passion, which may be conventional, that is, heterosexual, or it may, within a Turkish context, unofficial, forbidden, homosexual, pederastic, sadomasochistic, etc. Most often, a poem is both. If the passion is conventional, the *eda* tends to be direct, its melodic line echoing

---

*Ahmet Arif is as fine a poet as any belonging to the *Second New*. In fact, Turkish poets with strong Anatolian roots wrote poems independent from the *Second New*, not Istanbul obsessed, following a direct line from Nazım Hikmet.

the cadences of the *koşma*. If the passion is of a forbidden kind, the *eda* tends to move towards syntactical elaboration, experimentation, ambiguity. In fact, exploring the complexities of *eda* is the means by which the *Second New* poets introduce taboo themes, often sexual, into the public language.

Three major figures, in my opinion, dominate this poetic spectrum. Ece Ayhan is at one end. A poet of the victimized, of the totally discarded and forbidden, Ece Ayhan pushes the Turkish syntax overboard, so that words lose their linear context and explode from an unsettled center. *Eda* in Ece Ayhan is an elusive melody of pain, mourning and rage, punctuated by sparks of meaning. İlhan Berk is at the other end. The result of a curious, sponge-like mind, his poetry, often humorous, often delving in risqué themes, creates limitless variations in an idiosyncratic *eda*. Cemal Süreya is the central figure of the *Second New*. Though his subject is heterosexual love, its treatment is so full of the threat of a sense of loss that the total effect is thrilling and disturbing. Cemal Süreya makes startling new arrangements in the juxtaposition of images. At their best, these arrangements are unforgettable. They are Cemal Süreya's *eda*.

To understand Cemal Süreya's images is to understand the radical achievement of the *Second New* as a whole. *Eda* is the poetic embodiment of the Sufi spirit in the Turkish language. Cemal Süreya's image combinations are in fact the Sufi fusion of opposites, reconceived in the twentieth century. Cemal Süreya's erotic vision, pleasure relating to a loss of self, is Sufism stripped of religion, a secular mysticism. This Sufi aura (*eda*) permeates all of the *Second New*, even those poets who developed their work totally independently from Cemal Süreya. The simplest line in a satisfying *Second New* poem resonates with intimations beyond its actual sense. On the other hand, the most elaborate stylistic riff has a relentless underlying clarity. To understand why this is so, one must discuss a second idea besides *eda*, the treatment of Istanbul in the *Second New*.

Before going any further, I must clarify one point which may be an obstacle to a clear understanding of this poetry in the West. As Nazım Hikmet did to Mayakovsky, Cemal Süreya turned to French surrealism in search of his language. In fact, "In Your Country," in my opinion his greatest single poem, has elusive echoes of André Breton's "Union Libre." But Cemal Süreya ends somewhere completely different and new. André Breton's is about liberation; Cemal Süreya's is about the erosion of self, and liberation of a more than one thousand year old ethos from the blanket of history.

b) Istanbul: "I am listening to Istanbul with my eyes closed." —Orhan Veli

An amazing majority of the *Second New* poems take place in Istanbul. This is an obsessive relationship; specific scenes in poems — often love scenes — are located precisely. The *Second New* is permeated with place names.

There is a Turkish expression, "Ankara is a wife, Istanbul a mistress." Place names are specific locations in the body of Istanbul. In fact, Istanbul, like Sufism, has a profound contradiction attached to it. On the one hand, it is a city of unbelievable sensual beauty and clarity, of the Bosporus, water, gardens, minarets, etc. This side is often associated with the Islamic, official side of Istanbul. Istanbul is also a city of crooked streets, a maze. This side is associated with the geographically European side, specifically the Pera-Galata district, where European minorities, Orthodox Armenians and Greeks and Jews live. Pera/Galata is also the red light district of Istanbul, its denied underbelly. A specific name resonates with the part of the body which is being referred to, the visible or secret part.*

---

*On December 12, 1856, from his boat, seeing Istanbul (Constantinople), for the first time, Herman Melville sensed instinctively this erotic dimension, this mixture of the secret and the revealed, that Istanbul possesses: "The fog lifted from about the skirts of the city, which being built upon a promontory. . . . It was a coy disclosure, a kind of coquetting, leaving room for the imagination & heightening the scene. Constantinople, like her Sultanas, was thus veiled in her 'ashmack.'" (*Journals: The Writings Of Herman Melville*, vol. 15, edited by Howard C. Horsford with Lynn Horth [Evanston and Chicago: Northwestern University Press and The Newberry Library, 1989] p. 58) (*continued*)

Prior to the *Second New*, poetry deals with the official beauty of Istanbul. Cemal Süreya infuses it with danger by imposing the language and landscape of Sufism onto it. The gardens of Istanbul are also Pir Sultan's garden where "the rough men enter[s]." The Bosporus is also the brooks in Paradise. Its breathtaking harbor, the beginning of the Sea of Marmara, with its boats zigzagging between Europe and Asia, the Charon between life and death, across which Sufi poetry constantly crosses. The Galata Bridge, joining the

---

The journal Melville wrote during his twelve-day stay in *Constantinople* (pp. 58-68 of the *Journal*), obsessively tracing and retracing different parts of the city, particularly its Galata Bridge, trying to make a sense out of what he saw, with its sexual, possibly homosexual undertones, constitutes a *Second New* poem. In *Call Me Ishmael*, Charles Olson notices a connection between Melville's experiences of Istanbul and of the Pacific Ocean: "When he leans over the First Bridge [the Galata Bridge] his body is alive as it has not been since he swung with Jack Chase in maintops above the Pacific" (Charles Olson, *Call Me Ishmael: A Study of Melville* [San Francisco: City Light Books, 1947] p.95). Melville's journal of his stay has no overt references to the ocean or *Moby Dick*; the matter-of-factness of the writing, resisting symbolism, seeing the city in its own terms, full of place names, devoid of Western sentimentalities, is what makes it remarkable. Nevertheless, the allure of Constantinople as a "sultana," and the "sultanisms" ("The Specksynder," *Moby Dick*) of his obsessed, dictatorial Ahab, who drew charts of deeper, more cosmic oceanic currents, undreamt of by his more Western oriented Captain Starbuck, to meet his white whale, rejoin in the *eda* of these diaries. The Pacific and the Istanbul harbor connect in a continuous, meta-Western current. In my view, Melville responds instinctively to the mystical dimension of Istanbul because he sees it as an ambiguous space, of beauty and death and stench, cypresses inside graveyards, revelation and secrets, where lust for power and its consequent loss are joined with sexual lust. His Ahab inhabits the same psychic space, a suicidal, elusive revenge, as Cemal Süreya's seducer persona. Pip and the boys he meets in Istanbul are the same boys as in Ece Ayhan's poems. As Pip softens the "dictatorship" of Ahab's "innermost center, " the boys under the Galata Bridge touch Melville (isn't Melville's Holy Land pilgrimage a response by his family to his going mad after the writing of *Moby Dick*). Ahab too "had a wife and a child" (*Call Me Ishmael*, p. 61) before he went mad. Olson says Melville's response to Istanbul shows his emerging "spontaneity" (p. 95) to women; I am not so sure. As Pip is in *Moby Dick*, the little children under the Galata Bridge are the redeeming heart of the *Journals*, and not the "disappointment" (*Journals*, p. 91) of Jerusalem or the interminable poem he wrote during that time.

Melville responds to Istanbul with Ahab's "globular brain," as if he spoke Turkish, in broad sweeps. Nowhere is this clearer than in a startling passage in the *Journals* where in a mosque he senses Central Asian connections: "Went to Mosque of Sultan Sulyman. The third in point of size & splendor. — The Mosque is a sort of marble marquee of which the minarets (four or six) are the stakes. In fact when inside it struck me that the idea of this kind of edifice was borrowed from the tent." (p. 60). The madness of Ahab and Melville — as power, ego, pursuing their loss in destructive compassion — is Sufi, ecstatic. *Moby Dick* and *Journals* are the great Sufi works of the nineteenth century.

Islamic Istanbul with Pera, is another crossing. In Cemal Süreya's poetry Istanbul resonates as a mystical space.

The *Second New* poets can be defined by their locations in this same space. Ece Ayhan is the poet of Pera. His poetry is filled with Jewish, Greek, Armenian names, characters who are also eighty-year old prostitutes, molested children, homosexuals, sadists, etc; it is also filled with their sexually coded slang. As I mentioned, this vision is embodied in an extremely elusive syntax. Two events lie at the heart of this radically alienating verbal universe: a sister who committed suicide and a boy who was seduced. Ece Ayhan's *Miss Kınar's Waters* (1959) deals with the first; *A Blind Cat Black* (1965) with the second. The third book, *Orthodoxies* (1968), is an encyclopedia of the repressed and oppressed in the culture. Its title is a pun. On the one hand, it means Orthodox Christian, holy, righteous; as slang, it means its opposite, whore, perverse or untrue.

One distinction needs to be made between Cemal Süreya and Ece Ayhan. Cemal Süreya's poetry sees eros from the male side; seduction and eroticism of power lie at its heart. Ece Ayhan's poetry is the point of view of the victim and extends beyond sexuality to any kind of outcast state. Its theme is suffering and victimhood.

To the names of Cemal Süreya, Ece Ayhan and İlhan Berk, I must add Behçet Necatigil, who is not strictly speaking a *Second New* poet. His poetry deals with middle class, domestic life. But his interest in the undercurrents of this life leads him towards an elliptic language which has affinities with this group.

ʕʊ ʕʊ

The second part of my selection deals with the aftermath of the *Second New* and includes four poets, Özdemir İnce, Nilgün Marmara, Mustafa Ziyalan and Melisa Gürpinar. Though no unifying characteristics join them, certain trends are already clear: a) the obsessive focus on the body of Istanbul disappears; b) this generation includes women, Nilgün Marmara and Melisa Gürpinar, while the *Second New* was exclusively male; c) the focus among poets starts moving from Cemal Süreya to Ece Ayhan and Behçet Necatigil.

Özdemir İnce is the one with the closest contact with Cemal Süreya; but Cemal Süreya's obsessive style is replaced by a slower paced, meditative decorum. Nilgün Marmara's book *Typed Up Poems* (1988), written between 1977 and 1987, was followed shortly after by the author's suicide. The poems seem to be extensions of Ece Ayhan's *Miss Kinar's Water*, also a poem about a suicide. Full of word coinages and syntactical ambiguities, Nilgün Marmara's poems are both less abstract, more ego involved, and less precise than Ece Ayhan's. But, at their best, they create an abstract, melancholy music completely their own. Mustafa Ziyalan, an admirer of Behçet Necatigil, is involved in a language of subtexts. Finally, Melisa Gürpinar's *Istanbul's Eyes Are Cloudy* (1990) is my happy discovery, browsing in a bookstore in Istanbul. Among books after the *Second New*, hers is the only one I know which explores a new language for Istanbul. In startling narratives, often involving domestic tensions, the book concentrates on the slow extinction of people whose lives are inextricably bound with Istanbul's Ottoman style of living, a life which is inexorably disappearing. It is both strangely old fashioned and new, and, in my opinion, one of the most original poems of the last twenty years.

All the translations in the selection are my own. Translating these poems I tried to be faithful to the individual voice of each poet as much as I could. At the same time, certain consistent concerns underlay my endeavors. The intuitive nature of Turkish is always in tension for me with the syntactical fixity of English. In American English, in its ability to assimilate accents, I saw possibilities to bridge this gap. I hope I succeeded sometimes.

333

"Istanbul is not Constantinople." —Eartha Kitt

In "Waking to Constantinople" three names of the city of Istanbul interplay. The first is Byzantium, which was the name of the eastern part of the Roman Empire after its split. By its last gasp in the fifteenth century Byzantium had dwindled to the territory inside the city walls of its capital. Byzantium was the city itself; therefore, calling it Byzantium is referring to a dream like glory. The poem associates this dream with the color blue, the blue of the water surrounding the city.

The same blue surrounds the Tower of the Maiden (Kız Kulesi), which is a miniature white structure, a strange hybrid of a turret and a midget castle, built on a solitary rock right in the middle of the Istanbul harbor, taboo-like never stepped on but constantly visible. In the poem this blue whiteness is the linchpin to penetrate the city's dream past. Hardly mentioned by earlier poets, Kız Kulesi is an obsessive reference for the Turkish poets of the 1990's.

The second name is Constantinople, its historical name as a Christian city, the polis of Constantine, its founder, the first Christian Roman emperor. The Europeans kept referring to Istanbul as Constantinople until the establishment of the Turkish Republic in 1923.

The present name, Istanbul, is the name of Constantinople as a Moslem city, which it officially became after its conquest by the Ottomans in 1453. The derivation of the word is ambiguous. Istanbul may derive from Stambouli, which in Greek means "downtown." The first of the two times the poem uses the Islamic appellation, it spells it as "Stamboul," ironically pointing to its

Greek sources. A more officially acceptable derivation, possibly involving folk etymology, may be that "Istanbul" is a corruption of "İslam Bol" in Turkish, meaning "Full of Moslems."

"Waking to Constantinople" is a struggle between green (the green of Islamic rationality, scholarship, elegance, arabesque, exquisite beauty) and blue (blue of the innocent, primitive dream). The poem searches for a new name for the city, a synthesis which will involve the rational, official five-hundred year old Islamic side of Istanbul awakening to a much wider, older, decadent historical reality, which also loops back to its modern "decadence" of punk rock, motorcycles, etc.

A historical set of events underlie this search for a new synthesis. In the 1970's Istanbul was an exquisite, graceful city of about one and a half million people, which had also an underground life of perversions, etc., usually centered on Galata, its European side. All the Turkish poets of the twentieth century, including Orhan Veli and the poets of the *Second New* (Cemal Süreya, Ece Ayhan, etc) take this geographic, political and psychic structure as given, emphasizing one or the other of its sides. Melville refers to the same contrast of erotic beauty and stench, describing the city in his *Journals*. By the 1990's Istanbul had become a megalopolis, an urban sprawl of twelve million, the process destroying not only a huge number of its architectural jewels but also its psychic, linguistic structure. A self-contained body of contrasts became an unnamed continuum, making the poetic language of the 1960's and 1970's useless for contemporary conditions.

"Waking to Constantinople" searches for a new language by imagining its present sprawl as a dream-like historical sprawl which goes back three thousand years, seeing the contemporary deforming of the city as part of a historical continuum where the city was destroyed many times, realizing that the city's psychic and cultural energy — its geographic locus — is much more potent than any buildings which embody it. The girl who "dances the hula-hoop" is the same girl who has the "Byzantium dream with Lions."

The poem is itself the synthesis between green and blue it is looking for. The haunting arabesque convolutions of its melody, the Möbius-like turns of its arguments, uttered in Turkish and based on the Sufi aesthetics of *eda*, project a Byzantine dream argument which seems to deny it. The poem sprawls and dances at the same time, shedding names but remaining the same.

A MOMENT PLEASE:
küçük İskender's Preface to
cangüncem [*souljam*]

translated by Mustafa Ziyalan

The pseudo-poems in this collection, visions, images, vistas, unstudied for-
mulations, experimental notes and delusions are all, with an equally haphazard
sleight of hand, harvested from my *souljams* which have been written,
scribbled in an *improvised* fashion.

Similarities occasionally found between chapters, repetitions and
disruptions stem from the fact that most of my sensibilities, persons these
sensibilities are directed to and the relationships experienced in the process are
excluded from this society. Also, the books have been transcribed in a reverse
chronological order; an attempt has been made to suppress the chronological
confusion, to push it to the very beginning, to a fetal sensibility. For the in-
terested, the time frames within which the entries were made are enclosed in
their correct order.

Every misstep is put under protection!

I deliberately skipped certain names in my world. This is a result of my
concern to define myself by my desires.

There are four reasons why a work like this is being published:

1. To convey to the reader first-hand, by subjective censoring, the honest —
extreme — points some ideas had reached because of overwhelming weak-
nesses.

2. To validate the principle I stubbornly defended all the time, that "the *private* life of a writer, who has opened up to the reader, should be used as the main grounds to interpret what he has put forward."

3. To help illustrate the "graph in between" which would make easier for readers and interested critics to discuss my argument that "although I write in Turkish I am outside Turkish poetry," which I spelled out in an interview.

4. To eliminate the dilemma which would arise regarding whether or not to publish the "journals" in an edited form following a possible death.

Welcome to my life.

—kücük İskender (Alexander the little)

May 1994, Istanbul

SOULJAM/CANGÜNCEM:
küçük İskender's Subjectivity

The Motions of Infinite Love

Souljam is a big bang from the center of the soul, soul fragments —
"pseudo-poems . . . vistas, unstudied formulations, experimental notes and
delusions," as küçük İskender calls them in his introduction — pulling away
from each other, while they yearn for a faetal or necrophilic unity. Existence, in
souljam, is a series of explosions from and towards voids: "no man finally dies
because at his birth the umbilical cord is cut" (*cangüncem*, #646).

Violence is the pervasive catalyst in this process, in love, structure and lan-
guage. The lover's body in fragments through brutality, its missing emptiness
elicits a yearning for union. The cadences of this spiritual yearning — an *eda*
unto death, of fragments infused with intimations of completeness — constitute
the melody of the poem: "wounded electricity completes the body" (*souljam*,
#1)

is there any
lover of whose *hands hands only* statues are made,
oh, thine incorporeal hands! (*souljam*, #55)

İskender's Sufism

Sufism necessitates the break down of the ego for the soul to enter its ascent towards God. In küçük İskender's Sufism, the break down is in the lover's physical body, the orgasmic point of his up-your-face sexuality. The ego does not break; to the contrary, remaining intact, constitutes the subjectivity within which the break down occurs. What the speaker is yearning, "jamming" for in *souljam* is the faetal/fatal limits of his explosive subjectivity, the infinite contours of his consciousness. İskender's consciousness is God in his Sufism:

> in a utopia where suicide is unknown
> i'd like to settle as the god of suicide. (*cangüncem*, #646)

∾ ∾

> The rough man entered the lover's garden
> It is woods now, my beautiful one, it is woods,
> Gathering roses, he has broken their stems
> They are dry now, my beautiful one, they are dry
> —Pir Sultan Abdal (sixteenth-century Turkish Sufi poet)

Violence (in spirituality and love) is at the heart of the Sufi sensibility, part of its Shamanistic, intuitive synthesis. küçük İskender exploits, radicalizes the pagan essence of Sufism, its subversive ambiguity: the intimate link between God and self-destruction (sacrifice), sex and violence, love and death, religious fervor and political rebellion.

In Islamic Sufism, violence is sublimated as a cosmic principle, partly, through the dialectics of *arcs of ascent* and *descent*. God's unity breaks, dissipates into phenomenal multiplicity, while the broken down consciousness/ yearning soul needs, through weeping, wine, sacrifice, etc., to re-enter a climb back to unity, to God. This psychic transformation (rather, simultaneity) between descent and ascent — a jump, a mystical "sleight of hand" — is the focus of a lot of Sufi poetry, from Rumi to Hafız to a few young Turkish poets writing in the last decade of the twentieth century.

This moment of transformation is essentially subjective, of the mind's eye. İskender radicalizes this subjectivity by casting out the validity/reality of the outside world altogether, implying that, in its most subversive extension, in Sufism, man's mind is his God. Paradoxically, in this mysticism of completely of the mind, bound only by the psychic curvatures of birth and death (a kind of Einsteinian space) , he creates a text which is central, open-ended, inherently translatable.

Souljam in a Continuum

küçük İskender's poem is inherently translatable because of its intensely subjective universe. To understand this contradiction, one must go to its origin.

Souljam is a translation of küçük İskender's *cangüncem* (1996), itself a translation of the journal he kept, in twenty note-books, from February 19, 1984 to December 26, 1993. The poem reverses the order of the note-books, the lowest numbered fragments in *cangüncem* deriving from the chronologically latest note-book (#20), etc. Though basic themes and images remain the same, the chronological reversal utterly alters *cangüncem* from its time-bound, "journal" original. İskender describes the reason for the reversal in the following way:

an attempt . . . to suppress the chronological confusion, to push it to the very beginning, to a faetal sensibility.

Cangüncem records a faetal/fatal movement of the soul within the curvatures of total subjectivity, while the journal records ideas, images within the flow of time. This soulful movement *contra* time is the new thing *cangüncem* adds while "translating," crossing the linguistic void from the note-books to the poem.

In his introduction, İskender lists precisely which note-book provides the material for which block of fragments, e.g., book #20 (written between 31/8/92 and 26/12/93) for numbers 1-81, book #19 (written between 11/9/91 and 30/8/92) for numbers 81-206, etc. But, within each group, his translation rearranges, adds to and deletes from (he calls it "harvests") the entries. This process transforms a social language (collage), of philosophies, observations, lyric poems, etc., into an intensely private, counter-productive language moving in a space of the mind's eye, parallel to and defying social space, and which can not escape its subjectivity, but "arcs" within its limits. Within it, the descending order of the notebooks (from #20 down) evokes a progress towards simplicity. During the nine years of the writing of the journal, İskender's language moves towards greater ellipsis, in the earlier years echoing, among others, Orhan Veli's lyrical simplicity. As a result, paradoxically, *cangüncem's* subjectivity seems to include the history of the Turkish *eda* in the twentieth century. A subjectivity which implies a continuum within it outside itself.

İskender's eclectic language bursts with pop references, scientific terminology, phrases from newspaper crime reports, words with Sufi undertones, archaisms, philosophical rationalizations, lyric outbursts, etc. *Cangüncem* bares the psychic unity among the explosive fragments, the intuitive, compulsive connections below the rational level, the nerve-ending authenticity of İskender's subjectivity. This cadence, this melody, this *eda* of subjectivity — absent in the journals but present in the poem — begs to be re-translated. *Cangüncem* is replete with, in Walter Benjamin's definition, "translatability," that is, a text so inherently alien that the host language must move with the other into a third realm of "ideal language." The *eda* of *cangüncem* can not cross over but must implode into, grow within the subjectivity of a parallel translation, in a continuum of translations.

Souljam translates the first eighty-one fragments of canguncem (originally, notebook #20). It tries to reincarnate the unstudied eclecticism and destructive fertility of İskender's mind and language. This subjectivity can not be translated, but must grow from within the parallel universe of *souljam*; fragments need to be rearranged, references altered, as it happens between the note-books and the Turkish poem. There are no specific references to *Calvin Klein* (#3) or to Hitchcock's psycho (#47) in *cangüncem*, despite its many gay icons and film references. *Souljam* focuses on the *eda* of İskender's mind/soul — Walter Benjamin's realm of ideal language — the global, mysterious, unifying cadence of its explosive multiplicity. *Calvin Klein* and *psycho* are part of that cadence in its American reincarnation. *Cangüncem* becoming a violent jamming of the soul, a jam session of the soul, almost random, improvised.

Souljam remains an open-ended poem. It can be added to, compressed or rearranged as *cangüncem* was. *Souljam* too begs to be retranslated. Here lies the stunning openness of İskender's subjectivity. Despite his claims to being a peripheral writer, İskender's nihilistic explosiveness — the black hole eclecticism of his consciousness — paradoxically, creates a central text which crosses cultural and historical lines — from Turkish Sufism to Buddhism, to post-modern pop — into the future. It represents a nexus of continuous reincarnations, each begging to re-enunciate itself: "in solitude, me, full of hard ons ons and ons" (*souljam* #18).

AHMET GÜNTAN'S ROMEO AND ROMEO: The Melody of Sufi Union

Ahmet Güntan's *Romeo and Romeo* is a love poem between two men —
the title is the only clue to that — in which the lovers attempt to enter each
others' sleep to reach a mystical union. The five sections of the poem follow
the steps in the sleep process: "The Hour of Sleep," "Lullaby," "Sleep,"
"Dream," "The Hour to Wake Up."

Obstacles are hinted at during this pursuit of absolute union. The sleep and
wake-up times of the two appear out of sync with each other, one waking up
exactly when the other is going to sleep; there is also the hint of a third person
involved, a "he" or "she" or "it" (no gender distinction or distinction between
animate and inanimate exists in Turkish). In the melody/argument of the poem,
"I" argues that the logical impossibility of being at two places at the same time
can be transcended in the loving act of penetrating another's sleep because in
this act one turns into the other person. Looking for the other, one finds
oneself: "I'm with myself, alone, for myself,/ walking around, me, taking you
out,/ who, u-turning, takes within you, me" ("Dream").

Entering another's sleep is both an erotic and philosophical endeavor,
related to the Sufi concept of *arc of ascent*, the process (also a curve, a melody)
by which the distances among the elements fuse themselves into One Divine
Light. This erotic yearning is also a movement of the mind, towards justice, the
purified simplicity of mathematics. In the final two lines of the poem, Romeo
and Justice become one: "Justice Romeo!//Justice, my Romeo!" ("The Hour to
Wake Up")

344

Quite small in vocabulary, Turkish has a "radial" tendency, different meanings and grammatical functions converging, collapsing into the same words, sounds. The poem exploits this tendency, turning itself into the sound of Sufi union, the melody of the *arc of ascent*. Its intentionally minimalist vocabulary creates infinite variations, few words echoing and circling around each other, pulling towards a center: "Sleep with me, you,/in sleep you depart, from me,/in sleep I forget, I, I/depart from you." ("Sleep")

Economy is at the heart of Turkish literature, of that aspect which has Central Asian, pre-Islamic connections. Sufism has similar roots. *Romeo and Romeo* echoes the rhythms of the thirteenth-century Sufi folk poet, Yunus Emre. One might call *Romeo and Romeo* a gay spiritual written at the start of the third millennium.

This spirituality is anti-western, anti-modern — if one takes these terms to mean what has happened after the Renaissance in the West. It builds a bridge between ideas implicit in Arnold Schønberg and John Cage and traditions outside the West — specifically Islam, which was the ideological antagonist of the West until the sixteenth-seventeenth centuries. With roots in Plato, believing in the spirituality of colors and design, the Moorish and Sufi strains of Islam absolutely believe in the unity between the mind and the senses. Cartesian duality and its variations are inconceivable. In fact, embodiments of the *arc of ascent* are exercises of denial of this duality. It is this historical, intellectual challenge which makes Ahmet Güntan's poem and the works of a few other Turkish poets around him (Lale Müldür, Sami Baydar, Seyhan Erözçelik, küçük İskender, Enis Batur) so exciting and of such great value.

SOME NOTES ON *EDA*

by Mustafa Ziyalan

It was my mother who first introduced me to the concept of eda. Her name was Fatma Süzme Afyonlu and she was a poet in her own right, appreciated by none other than Nihat Sami Banarlı and anthologized up until 1965. She was closely familiar with folk and religious traditions in poetry.

Eda, in an everyday sense, means allure, particularly of a woman, or perhaps the presentation of allure. An expression like "with a lot of *eda*" would mean something like "with a self-conscious allure," bordering on "flirtatious."

I came to appreciate *eda* first as a rather concrete expression of the attitude, stance, sometimes even position of a poet, or of a particular poem. It was said that my mother, as a poet, had a "manly *eda*," for example. (A friend pointed out that *eda* usually needs a qualifier. I'd agree; outside the poem, it usually does.) Later, when I began reading Orhan Veli Kanık, I became acutely aware of an essence, which would make or break a poem, some element which was hard to nail down and describe. That was when I turned again to the concept.

In the work of a poet like Nazım Hikmet *eda* is rather obvious. His poetry has a point of view, an almost physical stance, and a way of relating itself. *Eda* here is perhaps the poetic "tone" or "attitude," a sustained, consistent, solid sense of stance (which may bring the Brechtian concept *gestus* to mind). I became first familiar with this kind of *eda* in Turkish poetry; an *eda* which emanates from the poet's and the poem's position, if not location.

Later, however, I became increasingly aware of the ever present yet overall more elusive qualities of *eda*. For that, I had to come to a more comparative understanding of Turkish language and poetry and their particular way of interacting.

ᖚ   ᖚ

Turkey is a country which is in many ways located — if not caught — in between: between Asia and Europe, between East and West, between the Ottoman Empire and Republic of Turkey, between fundamentalism and secularity, between colorful diversity and monochrome restraint, if not outright oppression. This pervasive feeling of being in between, dislocated, uprooted in one's own country — which is a reality to the people caught up in migration — is an essential ingredient of the mood often palpable in the country.

Similarly, Turkish language is located — this time — between the written and the spoken, perhaps with more emphasis on the latter. The Western alphabet was introduced in 1928. Readership is still low in numbers. The relative dominance of the spoken language is illustrated by the language's overall reliance on context, perhaps most importantly on social context; not only who says what, but also when, where, to whom are still very important, perhaps more so than it is in Western languages.

The break with the past which for better or worse came about with the demise of the Ottoman Empire and the foundation of the Republic in 1923 left some words which were reintroduced, resurrected or simply introduced into Istanbul Turkish, the dominant language of written poetry, devoid of a cumulative, complex content. Turkish has been increasingly infiltrated by foreign languages, which has further limited the growth and vascularization of it. These shifts may have left some words or to some extent all words as almost blank canvases, almost as smoke screens which one could venture to fill with one's own projections, and may have forced words to mean more, to have more than one meaning.

Turkish is an agglutinative language. The word or the component of the sentence closest to the verb carries the strongest emphasis and relevance in the sentence; beyond this the syntax is quite liberal compared to most Western languages; there is almost always a way of extracting meaning from a sentence regardless of the order of its components.

These qualities of the language empower a single word to have a level of autonomous functioning unknown in Western languages; for example, "nevyorklulaştıramadıklarımızdansınız" means "you are one of those we could not turn into a New Yorker." This is a single word with the function and meaning of a whole sentence. This has numerous consequences for poetry, enabling one, among other things:

1. to utilize a syntax which is considerably more flexible than the English one,

2. to use fewer words to tighten the poetic structure,

3. to use a single word as a line more effectively, without necessarily compromising the poetic richness.

Eda has been one of the most important, yet most elusive components of the structure in and the context around Turkish poetry, in my view perhaps the most important one holding everything together.

I ultimately came to acknowledge that in some other, less obvious ways eda harks back to the pagan, pantheistic roots of the peoples of Turkey, to a time when writing was a collective, anonymous gesture, creating almost the Zen in letters in an unconscious and ultimately doomed effort to overarch gaps, breaks and contradictions, to create a final yet ever elusive equilibrium. It is like the ingredient in jazz which makes jazz what it is. It is, according to the poet Simon Pettet, what makes Orhan Veli's poetry what it is. It lends itself immensely to helping poetry germinate in unexpected directions.

Coming back to my friend's point: I believe, as much as its eda is the qualifier of a poem, none other than the poem itself is the qualifier of its *eda*.*

---

*I am thankful to Semih Fırıncıoğlu, Dalia Kandiyoti and as always, to Pınar Ziyalan for their constructive remarks about this text.

NOTES ON A TURKISH TRIP:
The Sights and Colors of Turkey

What are things which differentiate Turkey?

a) An obsession with view and location. Most inland restaurants and tea houses are located in a place with trees. Shade has a hint of paradise to a Turk. Every restaurant is a resting place, therefore, is under a shade, quiet, a respite from the steppe, from the treeless plain, ideally, a pool with fish in it.

If near the water, the restaurants huddle around the water, extend into it, as wooden quays, etc., and get built there. Resting starts with looking into the water, then the evening comes, the lights reflected into the water, turning violet, then the lights in the city, then the music, dolorous, strumming, mournful, then the food, beer, raki.

If not at the water, restaurants turn to it, across the road perhaps, on a raised platform, under trees, lights strung from hanging ropes, little shades of paradise overlooking the view.

There is a tea house at the back end of a public park, Gülhane Park (Park of Roses), which used to be grounds belonging to the Topkapı Palace. The park overlooks the Istanbul harbor, which is constantly crossed by white, yacht size commuter boats, as if a plaza. All the chairs in the tea house were turned (this special day we were there), from this height towards the harbor, along a parapet. Only tables along it were occupied. Couples (this was a family tea house and no single man or woman was allowed to use it) or families with kids, mother-in-laws, etc., sat there, a pot of tea or soda bottles on the table. Very

349

few spoke to each other, including kids, but sat their chairs turned to the water and watched the view, occasionally taking a sip, whispering, a song composed a hundred years ago with the *ud* and drums playing in the background. Music, view, tea, wind, silence. A respite of contemplative peace, yearning as pleasure, history, momentarily, grazing you with a feather weight, embracing you as an eternal lover — all the while the languishing of white boats between Europe and Asia; the very spot which was Herman Melville's first view of the city also:

The fog only lifted from about the skirts of the city, which being built upon a promontory, left the crown of it hidden wrapped in vapor. Could see the base and wall of St. Sophia but not the dome. It was a coy disclosure, a kind of coquetting, leaving room for the imagination & heightening the scene. Constantinople, like her Sultanas, was thus veiled in her "ashmak." —Herman Melville, *Journals*

A melancholy plethora of the senses — at the secret heart of Istanbul. Seeing as a medium of being.

The garden still plethora, with your sweetest voice
If one day you long back oh for a station of that summer

Look at the nodding water of the harbor, you'll see,
That past night lying in its depth
                    —Yahya Kemal Beyatlı, "That Summer"

b) In the United States, in our time, pastel, the opposite of loud, is the color of taste, a vision of subtle suggestions, proud, self-conscious understatement around which beauty ("skinny" is also a vision of the pastel, a Puritanical understatement of the body) and peace are organized. In Turkey, if one moves away from Istanbul, particularly into central Anatolia, one realizes that the center of Turkey is an extremely dry and, until recently, barren country. An unending, arid vision of sun-blasted land, of the pastel. That's why the Turkish love of trees forming a shade. Earth tones, unsoftened by green, is not a Ralf Lauren vision of style in Anatolia, but a cruel historical fact, an agent of denial. This creates ironies which are difficult, for an American for instance, to understand, which appear as negatives, defects; but nevertheless are ingrained in the Turkish soul and taste.

Anatolian peasant women wear fiery clothing — often reds, pinks, purples — working in the fields, so striking since Islam asks women to cover themselves in tent size gray or black coats in the street. Western rug dealers, who love Turkish designs, must negotiate, by hook or crook, often through bleaching, around this Anatolian impulse for the primary.

Equally, the Elgin Marbles (named after their aristocratic thief — Lord Elgin — who stripped them white for his ideal of the Greek) were colorful, obscene glories in the pediments of the Acropolis.

Tourist roads on the Aegean are lined with displays of mostly mauve pottery of spectral dimensions. Who would buy them, in which house can one place this still unforgettable aggression of color was the question I kept asking myself.

from PORNOGRAPHY OF THE IMAGE* *by ZEYNEP SAYIN*

translated by Saliha Paker

Ibn al-'Arabî, who traveled in the thirteenth century from Andalusia to Anatolia, wrote that the Byzantines had perfected pictorial art because, in their icons, Jesus Christ's unique nature was fused with the concept of unity (*tevhid*). The icon is capable of achieving this fusion because it is the mirror of the invisible, not the visible. Coming from a Muslim thinker and mystic, such words may at first seem strange, but they are not so surprising if one considers that in Anatolia the first examples of script-pictures, or images created by Arabic writing, began to emerge during the thirteenth century. All such images were organized in order to be read, so that the letter would be delivered to the eye, rather than merely made visible. From this perspective, writing signifies picture and, like Anatolian "script-pictures," Byzantine icons ask to be read in fragments and in sections. As also implied by the Greek verb *graphein* and the Russian *pisat*, which mean "write" and "engrave" respectively, the icon is not a picture but an ideograph which needs to be read through figures instead of letters. In this context, image and sign are identical, as are picture and letter : the universe is a form of writing which draws its existence from the Divine Word; *graphem* or *letter* transmits the magical power of the Word in different ways, thus avoiding the separation of script from picture, or sign from image.

İmgenin Pornografisi (Istanbul: Metis Publishing , 2003)

Indeed Ibn al-'Arabî's thinking postulates both the premise for and the culmination of Anatolian scriptural figurations. With his intellectual thrust, the conception of purity (in the sense of exemption from defect or accidence) which is inherent in Islamic thinking on the *Kur'an*, evolves into something beyond that. Purity becomes a quality whereby divine transcendence is held above any likeness and exempt from any attribution of likeness. Especially in Sunni Islam, nothing in the universe is considered equal to or 'like' *Allah*. Contrary to the principle of similitude in the modern age, the visible is not 'like' the invisible. The distinction introduced by Heidegger which, he argued, was forgotten by Western metaphysics, has always been valid in Islamic thinking on the *Kur'an*: being is held free (*münezzeh*) of any attribution of likeness because the "essence" of being cannot be equated with what exists. In a sense, this is what Heidegger called "ontic-ontological" difference, or what Ibn al-'Arabî termed *furkan*, a derivation from the root-word *fark* (difference). While, in one respect, the whatness of being is *in* that which exists and in a more intimate relationship than that between the aorta and the human body to which it belongs, in another respect, this whatness is exempt from any image of that which exists. Thus, it is not possible to establish a relationship between the essence of being and the 'how' or the 'likeness' of that which exists on the basis of the principle of similitude that defines Western metaphysics. Neither is it possible to represent the farness of the transcendent principle by means of any 'likeness' or comparison. This way of thinking claims that eyes do not reconstruct what they see when looking, that they cannot reach divinity; it admits that the absoluteness of the transcendent law cannot be comprehended only on the basis of vision. That which exists is the mirror of the invisible, not the visible. Instead of directing the gaze to the locus of manifestation where the divine being reveals itself, the eye must become passive to the point of being incapable of looking anymore. Likewise one must attain such passivity that one removes oneself from the gaze — the point at which there is nothing left of the self but divine law.

Letters that form the scriptural figurations are not connecting elements, so to speak, between invisibility and visibility; instead they connect something that is itself virtual — the letter which is the word's image — with a another virtuality. Since the aim is to protect divine invisibility, the rift between the divine unknowable and the letters is formed by a chain of complex connections. Divinity masks itself with its own writing; thus it avoids delivering to the gaze even the *what*ness of its mask. The locus of manifestation is an image that pursues divinity's traces; it is also the divine's other. The world of appearance that writes the divine text is a *similitude dissimilar* to what lies behind that world. This similitude assumed a *double existence* after the thirteenth century.

Both in the icons and in the script-pictures, a veil is posed between the visible and the invisible. Both forms of knowledge are 'ashamed' to deliver the invisible to the gaze. In many post-thirteenth century narratives inspired by Ibn al-'Arabî, the reason for shame, or (in Islamic terminology) *hijab*, is explained in terms of the universe being read as a sign that reveals the *sırr*, the mystery of the transcendent. The Arabic word *sırr* in this context signifies not only the mystery, the absolutely invisible volume and depth of the transcendent body, but also the invisible behind the mirror. Because the universe that pursues the trace of the divine touch is viewed as the exhibition of divinity's shame, to gaze upon it is as shameful as looking upon a naked body. For this reason Ibn al-'Arabî defines the manifest world in terms of *fevahiş*. This is an Arabic word which signifies not only a sense of shame, a shameful act, blame or sin, but also the exposing or exhibiting of oneself.

In fact, as divine secrecy is concealed from the eye by what Ibn al-'Arabî called the "illusive veil," it imposes a distance or space between the visible and the invisible, thus reminding the eye of its limits and how far it can look. The distance between the gaze and the eye is one that is imposed because it befits the human — a pronouncement of the *Kur'an* with respect to the invisible world and the world of appearance. The human being possesses no knowledge of the illusive veil, let alone the invisible world. Interestingly, in visual representations characteristic of Anatolia, the "image" springs from the background. But the invisible background is twice removed from the front, twice doubled by the distance of the *figura* and the letter, because the *figura* is twice as far from the invisible on account of the space and abstraction inherent in the letter itself. For this reason, this is an image which can no longer be qualified as an image. If, as Heidegger stated, the primary function of an image is to transmute the invisible into the visible, then, in this case, the image has no such function. What unites the specifically Anatolian sign and the Byzantine icon is the emphasis in both that the core of the real (*le réel* in the Lacanian sense) that is hidden in the visible differs from the visible. The image in a semiotic order has placed a double(d) uncleavable distance between what it signifies and what it cannot signify. But the same doubling applies to the distance between the image and the eye, and *hijab* is this distance, pushing away farther that which should remain invisible.

. . .

Contrary to general opinion, Anatolian art does not at all lack in figurative representations claimed to have been banned by Islam. From script pictures, which developed after the thirteenth century, to Ottoman miniatures, a variety of three-dimensional creatures and objects have been continuously represented in Anatolia, including the naked body. But such figures are of a semiotic nature: a distance must be allowed between the gaze and the eye, with regard to the distance already posed between the visible and the invisible.

Let me give a radical example. The *Ferhatname* by Arifî of Erdebil, which according to Malik Aksel is found in the Topkapı Palace Museum, seems to be trying to prove that pornography is not related to the exhibition of genitalia. The *Ferhatname* displays naked genitalia in various love scenes, but it is only the lovers' faces that shun the gaze. Because it is shameful for eyes to be fixed on faces and to expose what they conceal, the gaze is diminished. Even if nakedness invites the gaze so that it can meet the eye, the core of the "real" hidden in the face will never be captured. Even when it is veiled, or, by virtue of its being veiled, the core of the "real" looks back at the onlooker. For this reason, the face, which symbolizes the body's soul, is expressionless when unveiled in Ottoman miniatures: the face masks the visibility of the soul; it responds to the onlooker's gaze by springing from the mask. In view of this, if one needs a Turkish word for *resim* (borrowed from Arabic to mean 'picture') that word should be *kılık* (guise).The signs that deliver to the eye the manifestation, or the "guise," that is the image of the invisible, veil that manifestation with *hijab*.

It is true that unveiled depictions of prophets are rare, both in Anatolia and Persia. Nevertheless, we do encounter such examples. Sacred figures of Bektaşî and Hurufî origin, particularly those bearing Persian influence, have played a part in shaping ways of Anatolian representation. In mosques and other locations saintly figures and holy personages are represented by script-pictures. This is the way of delivering to the eye, "in the form of a *Kur'an* in motion," the abstract similitude of Allah's name by inscribing it in its abstraction. According to a saying of the Prophet, sacred letters may be read on the human face because the *Kur'an* and the human being are twins.While the faces of the Prophet Ali or of Fazl-ı Hurufî are not images like icons, made for hanging on the wall, they nevertheless share a common feature: both are based on the principle of a likeness that is not alike. Both in the case of the script-picture and the icon, because the pictorial surface is not of the kind that is organized to show proximity or distance, or smallness or magnitude, in order to satisfy the gaze, one cannot speak of a figure — background opposition that is posed by a central perspective. On the contrary, what is privileged in both cases, is not the figure but the background that constitutes the figure, which even inserts the distance pertaining to the letters, and which, in terms of space, is never filled. The figure serves as a means for foregrounding the background. Everything is shaped by that background which is protected from visibility. Despite all the differences between them, it is this characteristic that unites the icon and the script-picture: neither is a window that opens to the eye. This signifies that the script-picture "positions the figurative narrative in the temporality of a sacred space" instead of opening up the image, for an instant, to the realm of the perspectival frame in the modern manner after Alberti and Brunelleschi. The common feature of all Byzantine mosaics in Ravenna and elsewhere is the *figura* itself. The *figura*'s "existence" is not organized according to the figure-background principle characteristic of the Renaissance; it does not have to "be proved by a systematically defined space," nor can spatial existence fix the stance of the figure. In this way, in script-pictures and in miniatures parts of the figure which, from a central perspective, would be invisible, will be visible from a reverse perspective, as, for instance, in the Byzantine icons in which the back of the head can be seen as well as the face, the nape as well as the neck, the hair parting which can only be viewed from above as well as the fringe visible from the front, or the long nose as observed from above the head as well as from the front. All such images are governed by a multicentredness which prevents the eye from fixing on a single focal point. Instead of the eye directing itself at the picture from a single central point, it is the multicentred picture, just like the icon, that opens out to the eye, divides the eye's angle, and instead of familiarizing it, misleads. In script-pictures and miniatures, different centers of focus bestow on the eye a strange activeness that, obviously, is not offered an infinite number of options. Nevertheless, the eye, directed by whatever options available, can shift back and forth among the different angles of the image, constantly diminishing the gaze which desires to be fixed. The image deliberately surprises the gaze and forces it to shifting positions.

ARE TURKS REALLY. . . DANGEROUS?

an interview with Lale Müldür by Fatih Özgüven
translated by Saliha Paker

Lale Müldür is writing a novel. For those of us who like her writing, such news is enough to spark curiosity. I kept quiet for a change and simply asked her my questions.

FÖ: What are you writing about?

LM: About Istanbul, of course. But a different Istanbul, my own. This is how I see it. It is evident from the title of the novel, *Byzansiyya*, which I've come up with fusing "Bizans" [Turkish adaptation of the French "Byzance" for "Byzantium"] with "Konstantiniyya" [the Muslim name for Constantinople before its conquest by the Ottomans]. To arrive at Istanbul's true name, I had to mix the East and the West. Part of the action takes place in Istanbul, the holy city, which has also been known as "Nova Roma," "Byzantion" [Byzantium], "Konstantiniyya" and "Tzarigrad." What makes it feel like Istanbul or Constantinople is something in its air. A strange electricity. Like a spiritual centre, it keeps shifting between the East and the West, changing hands. On the Surrealists' map, for instance, there are only two capitals: Istanbul and Paris. I sensed Istanbul's electricity most in a Transglobal Underground concert I attended abroad. The singer was of Arab-Jewish-English background, a woman of extraordinary charisma who combined techno and North African music."We

358

are the dirty underpants of world fusion," the group said. Similarly, Istanbul is a site of strange fusions.

FÖ: Did you do any research for the book?

LM: Yes, I had to do it, to place Istanbul exactly. In the novel, Istanbul once more stands at the forefront of global conflict , the crossroads of world history. To the Byzantines, the Virgin Mary protected the city, even personally fighting alongside those defending it. The calendars of Constantinople's churches were full of feasts devoted to the Virgin Mary. The Byzantines believed the city would be protected against aggression because it was a fortress of Christianity. A similar image in reverse is conveyed in a holy saying of the Prophet of Islam: "Konstantiniyya will surely be conquered one day." With the discovery of Eyup's grave, Istanbul also becomes the holy city of Islam. The Hagia Sophia seems to have held a key position in the multilayered imperial history of the city, in the chain of struggles over her. It is interesting that during the siege of Constantinople by the Ottomans, the people, including the emperor, gathered in the Hagia Sophia. Why did they do so? When the city fell, the first thing the Conqueror [Sultan Mehmet II] did was to kneel at the marble altar of the Hagia Sophia and face Mecca to perform his first prayer. The Hagia Sophia seems to have been at the heart of things right up to this day, even for the Byzansiyyans in my book. They are people who drink the liqueur of wisdom, of *sophia*, distilled from madness. They find a key inside the Hagia Sophia and a porphyrian year behind them.

FÖ: Perhaps for you it is not necessary, but how do you square this up with history?

LM: I combine Byzantine legends of long ago with a fictional story of our day, with an assumption almost mythological in its mystery. Links are made between our time and the foundation myths of Konstantiniyya and the Hagia

359

Sophia. But I don't want to talk about what happens in the story.

FÖ: Byzansiyyans are a different kind of people, aren't they?

LM: Yes. They belong to Byzansiyya, not to Istanbul. I don't want to decode the way I characterized them. All I can say here is that they figure in the novel like relics of Byzantium. These people can't live modestly like the Belgians, for instance. They look upon themselves as the chosen people, like the Jews. This is a "Byzantine" state of mind. Similarly, Moscow regards itself as the third Rome, an attitude the Russians inherited from Byzantium. In my account of Byzansiyyans, I was led also to psychoanalyze the Turks.

FÖ: What do you mean, exactly?

LM: For instance, it is rumored among angels that the eschatological role of the Turks was to conquer Constantinople. This raises a question: are Turks really . . . dangerous? In my novel, their challenge to conquer the West, starting with the conquest of Constantinople in 1453, turns into a dangerous project, dangerous psychological adventures, Ottoman megalomania needing to find itself a new niche in each Turk's subconscious.

FÖ: Is all this related to your previous work?

LM: I realized later on that the book had grown out of some of my poems, "Waking to Constantinople" from the *Book of Series* and "Héloise/ Hagia Sophia" and "Tzarigrad/Istanbul" from my first book of poetry, *Distant Storm*.

FÖ: Byzansiyyans are in deep trouble, aren't they?

LM: I don't want to get into that, but I can talk about a few points. Byzansiyyans are the most westward-looking Easterners. In Persian, the expression "to be westernized" also signifies receiving a blow from the West, getting sun-stroke. This is both positive, because it means absorbing sun-related values, and negative, implying that such values land on us like an avalanche. So you see, Byzansiyyans are sun-struck people. Even if each individual is a pathological case, one can at least say Byzansiyyans have drawn for themselves a "luminous path of escape," in the Deleuzian sense.

FÖ: Is there love in it?

LM: I can only say this much: the Byzansiyya axis is organized according to a principle of desire, integrating beauty and schizophrenia.

FÖ: In *Northern Notebooks* didn't you write poetry as fiction? What about *Byzansiyya*?

LM: *Northern Notebooks* was something like the *nouveau* roman. *Byzansiyya* is more like fiction as fiction.*

---

*Lale Müldür never finished *Byzansiyya* as a novel.

APPENDIX: TURKISH TITLES OF THE POEMS IN THE ANTHOLOGY

AHMET HAŞİM:
That Space (O Belde, *Göl Saatleri,* 1921)
Glass (Mukaddime, *Piyale,* 1926)
"In a grieving perfection's insomnia"(Bülbül, *Piyale,* 1926)
Ascension (Merdiven, *Piyale,* 1926)
"Out of the beloved's lip" (Karanfil, *Piyale,* 1926)
"A river of fire"(Parıltı, *Piyale,* 1926)

YAHYA KEMAL BEYATLI:
That Summer (Geçmiş Yaz, *Kendi Gök Kubbemiz* 1961)
Night (Gece, *Kendi Gök Kubbemiz,* 1961)
Reunion (Vuslat, *Kendi Gök Kubbemiz,* 1961)

FARUK NAFİZ ÇAMLIBEL:
The Escaper (Firari, *Çoban Çeşmesi,* 1926)

AHMET HAMDİ TANPINAR:
Whole Summer (Bütün Yaz, *Şiirler,* 1961)
Bar (Bir Gül Bu Karanlıklarda, *Şiirler,* 1961)
Roads Too Early (Yollar Çok Erken..., *Şiirler,* 1961)

NÂZIM HİKMET:
The Blue-eyed Giant (Mavi Gözlü Dev, Minnacık Kadın ve Hanımelleri, *Gece Gelen Telegraf,* 1932)
Poems of Twenty-One and Twenty-Two O'Clock (Saat 21-22 Şiirleri, *Saat 21-22 Şiirleri,* 1965)
The Night on August 26, 2:30 A.M. to 3:30 A.M., from *Human Landscapes from My Country* (*Memleketimden İnsan Manzaraları,* 2. kitap, 1966)

NECİP FAZIL KISAKÜREK:
"Neither the sick wait for morning"(Beklenen, *Sonsuzluk Kervanı,* 1955)
Gazel (Ben, *Sonsuzluk Kervanı,* 1955)
"Merciful boxy hotel rooms, smoky oil lamps, oil lamps"(Otel Odaları, *Kaldırımlar,* 1928)
"I am a wanderer on earth"(Serseri, *Yeni Mecmua,* 1924)
Fret (Çile, *Sonsuzluk Kervanı,* 1955)

SAİT FAİK:
The Man Who Did Calisthenics (Cimnastik Yapan Adam, *Havuz Başı,* 1952)
Maricula (Marikula Doğur, *Şimdi Sevişme Vakti,* 1953)

ASAF HÂLET ÇELEBİ:
"The lover is only one, but to look at herself"(Ayna, *He,* 1942) and the poet Seyhan Erözçelik's comments on the poem in Asaf Hâlet Çelebi, *Bütün Şiirleri,* haz. Seyhan Erözçelik, 1998)

362

H (He, *He*, 1942)
Uncle Sea Buoy (Şamandıra Baba, *Lâmelif*, 1945)
Maria (Mariyya, *Om Mani Padme Hum*, 1953)
A Manifesto of the Eye (Benim Gözümle Şiir Davası, Asaf Hâlet Çelebi, *Bütün Yazıları*,
haz. Hakan Sazyek, 1998)

ORHAN VELİ KANIK:
Quantitative (Quantitatif, *Bütün Şiirleri*, 1951)
Makes Me Dizzy (Efkârlanırım, *Garip*, 1941)
Exodus I (Hicret I, *Garip*, 1941)
My friend Sabri (Montör Sabri, *Bütün Şiirleri*, 1951)
Invitation (İstanbul İçin, *Garip*, 1941)
The Guest (Misafir, *Bütün Şiirleri*, 1951)
Birds Tell Lies (Kuşlar Yalan Söyler, *Garip*, 1941)
I Am Listening To Istanbul (İstanbul'u Dinliyorum, *Karşı*, 1949)
Suicide (İntihar, *Bütün Şiirleri*, 1951)
Trip (Seyahat, *Bütün Şiirleri*, 1951)
People (İnsanlar, *Varlık Dergisi*, 1937)
The Shameful Feelings Of A Bad Man (İş Olsun Diye, *Bütün Şiirleri*, 1951)
Ecstasy (İş Olsun Diye, *Bütün Siirleri*, 1951)
For The Hell of It (İş Olsun Diye, *Bütün Şiirleri*, 1951)
To Keep Busy (İş Olsun Diye, *Bütün Şiirleri*, 1951)
The Galata Bridge (Galata Köprüsü, *Karşı*, 1949)
The Parade of Love (Aşk Resmigeçiti, *Bütün Şiirleri*, 1951)

CELÂL SILAY:
"branch swings in the wind" (Kum Kumdan Başka Damla Damladan, *Doğa*, 1965)

OKTAY RİFAT:
Ancient Seals (Eski Mühürler, *Şiirler*, 1969)

MELİH CEVDET ANDAY:
The Pigeon (Güvercin, *Göçebe Denizin Üstünde*, 1970)

BEHÇET NECATİGİL:
Exam (Sınav, *Kareler Aklar*, 1975)
Frost (Kırağı, *Kareler Aklar*, 1975)
Ready Made (Hazır Giyim, *Kareler Aklar*, 1975)
House (Perili Ev, *Evler*, 1953)
Unsaid Love (Gizli Sevda, *Evler*, 1953)

CAHİT KÜLEBİ:
"Trucks carry melons" (İstanbul, *Adamın Biri*, 1946)
"Rosy lips" (Hikâye, *Adamın Biri*, 1946)

İLHAN BERK:
Time Of Hunting (Av Vakti, *Âşikane*, 1968)
Garden (Bahçe, *Şeyler Kitabı – Ev*, 1997)

363

Garlic (Sarmısak, *Kül*, 1978)
Homer's Commentators and Slaves (Homeros Yazıcıları ve Köleler, *Kül*, 1978)
Reading Li Po (Li Po'yu Okurken, *Kül*, 1978)
Neither Did I See Such Loves/Nor Such Partings (Ne Böyle Sevdalar Gördüm/Ne Böyle
Ayrılıklar, Köroğlu, 1955)
Jet-Black (Oltu Taşi, *Güzel Irmak*, 1988)
Fish Market, Backstage Street (Balıkpazarı, *Pera*, 1990)
The Denizens of the Arcade Hristaki (Hristaki Pasajı Sakinleri, *Pera*, 1990)

ARİF DAMAR:
The Broken Spool (Kırık Makara, *Seçme Şiirler*, 1998)

METİN ELOĞLU
Love Letter (Aşk Mektubu, *Düdüklü Tencere*, 1951)
The Address of Turkey (Türkiye'nin Adresi, *Türkiye'nin Adresi*, 1965)

TURGUT UYAR
A Virtuous Lady's Unfortunate Life (Salihat-i Nisvandan Saffet Hanımefendi'ye, *Dîvan*,
1970)

AHMET ARİF:
Notes from the Diyarbekir Fortress (Diyarbekır Kalesinden Notlar, *Hasretinden Parangalar
Eskittim*, 1968)
Thirty-three Bullets (Otuz Üç Kurşun, *Hasretinden Parangalar Eskittim*, 1968)
Leyli, My Leyli (Leylim – Leylim, *Hasretinden Parangalar Eskittim*, 1968)

CEMAL SÜREYA:
Houri's Rose (Gül, *Üvercinka*, 1958)
Dying In A Turkish Bath (Sizin Hiç Babanız Öldü Mü, *Üvercinka*, 1958)
"The woman stripped herself slowly" (Şiir, *Üvercinka*, 1958)
"The most beautiful woman, she was" (Yazmam Daha Aşk Şiiri, *Üvercinka*, 1958)
"Whereas a glass of water was enough to wet your hair" (Aşk, *Üvercinka*, 1958)
"They sheared the cloud, the cloud now is clear" (Dalga, *Üvercinka*, 1958)
The Apple (Elma, *Üvercinka*, 1958)
The Bee (Elma, *Üvercinka*, 1958)
Muezzin (Şu Da Var, *Üvercinka*, 1958)
Drizzle (Adam, *Üvercinka*, 1958)
"Whenever we threw a cigarette into the water" (Cıgarayı Attım Denize, *Üvercinka*, 1958)
In Your Country (Ülke, *Göçebe*, 1965)
Two Things (İki Şey, *Beni Öp Sonra Doğur Beni*, 1973)
Second is... (Yirmi Şiir, *Sevda Sözleri*, 1990)
Couplets (11 Beyit, *Sevda Sözleri*, 1990)
Photograph (Fotograf, *Uçurumda Açan*, 1988)
"Life is short"(Kısa, *Sevda Sözleri*, 1990)
"This government"(Hükûmet, *Sevda Sözleri*, 1990
"'Dying?' you said"(Göller Denizler, *Sevda Sözleri*, 1990)
"I'm dying, God"(Üstü Kalsın, *Sevda Sözleri*, 1990)
"After twelve P.M."(Şarap, *Sevda Sözleri*, 1990)

ECE AYHAN:
The Sultan With a Lily (Zambaklı Padışah, *Zambaklı Padışah*, 1981)
Miss Kinar's Waters (Kınar Hanımın Denizleri, *Kınar Hanımın Denizleri*, 1959)
Phaeton (Fayton, *Kınar Hanımın Denizleri*, 1959)
To Trace from Hebrew (İbraniceden Çizmek, *Kınar Hanımın Denizleri*, 1959)
Wall Street (Kambiyo, *Kınar Hanımın Denizleri*, 1959)
Spill (Bir Ölü Macar Cambaz, *Kınar Hanımın Denizleri*, 1959)
"And the Sirocco was born" (Ecegiller, *Kınar Hanımın Denizleri*, 1959)
"You have a smile, wicked, I'll grant you" (A. Petro, *Kınar Hanımın Denizleri*, 1959)
Mermaid Eftalia (Denizkızı Eftalya, *Kınar Hanımın Denizleri*, 1959)
A Tree Full of Songs (Kanto Agacı, *Kınar Hanımın Denizleri*, 1959)
Harbor (Gül Gibi Kanto, *Kınar Hanımın Denizleri*, 1959)
The Nigger In A Photograph (Bir Fotografın Arabı, *Bakışsız Bir Kedi Kara*, 1965)
Epitafio (Epitafio, *Bakışsız Bir Kedi Kara*, 1965)
Orthodoxies I (I, *Ortodoksluklar*, 1968)
Orthodoxies X (X, *Ortodoksluklar*, 1968)
Orthodoxies XV (XV, *Ortodoksluklar*, 1968)

GÜLTAN AKIN:
The Wedding and The Snow (Düğün ve Kar, *Sessiz Arka Bahçeler*, 1998)

ÖZDEMİR İNCE:
Sage (Ermiş, *Gündönümü Gündönümü*, 1992)
1968, Filled with Love (1968 Günleri, *Gündönümü Gündönümü*, 1992)
Stay With Me (Benimle Kal, *Gündönümü Gündönümü*, 1992)
Continuities (Günler ve Günler, *Gündönümü Gündönümü*, 1992)

MELİSA GÜRPINAR:
The Bank Teller Tecelli Bey (veznedar tecelli bey, "*İstanbul'un Gözleri Mahmur*, 1990)

ENİS BATUR:
Gloria (Gloria, *Gri Dîvan*, 1990)
Passport (Pasaport, *Gri Dîvan*, 1990)

AHMET GÜNTAN:
Romeo & Romeo (Romeo ve Romeo, *Romeo ve Romeo*, 1995)

LALE MÜLDÜR:
turkish red (turkish red, *Seriler Kitabı*, 1991)
turkish blue (turkish blue, *Seriler Kitabı*, 1991)
blauwviolet (blauwviolet, *Seriler Kitabı*, 1991)
Waking to Constantinople (Constantinopolis'e Uyanmak, *Seriler Kitabı*, 1991)
Virgin Mary's Smoke (Buhurmeryem, *Buhurmeryem*, 1994)
The Yellowing (üzünç, sevgilim ya da nane otları, *Voyicir 2*, 1990)
Are Turks Really... Dangerous? (türkler gerçekten... tehlikeli mi?, *anne ben barbar miyim?*, 1998)

HAYDAR ERGÜLEN:
Caramel (Karamela, *40 Şiir ve Bir...*, 1997)
Placid (Durgun, *40 Şiir ve Bir...*, 1997)

NILGÜN MARMARA:
"Love is a kilim"(Martının Altındaki Kilim, *daktiloya basılmış şiirler*, 1988)

MUSTAFA ZİYALAN:
Days (Sayılari saatleri sana göre tanımlamalı, *Dünle Yarın Arasında*, 1990)
Kumkapı, by the Sea (Kumkapılı Teyzeme, *Dünle Yarın Arasında*, 1990)
The Shape of Clouds (Zaman Ufacık Çocuk, *Dünle Yarın Arasında*, 1990)
Grandfather Clock (Kumkapılı Teyzeme, *Dünle Yarın Arasında*, 1990)
Oedipus De-boned (Ödipüs Rex, Karagümrük)
Isms (ölüm/çalar/saat)

SEYHAN ERÖZÇELIK:
"A dream in Istanbul of falling"(Düştanbul, *Kır Ağı*, 1991)
The hand drawing (a chart the poet Seyhan Erözçelik drew on a piece of paper at a coffee
shop in Istanbul to clarify the different words buried in his coinage "düştanbul."
"A dream in Istanbul of falling" is a translation of that chart.
Platonic (Eflatuni Aşk I & II, *Kır Ağı*, 1991)
Coffee Grinds (Kahve Falı, *Gül ve Telve*, 1997)

SAMİ BAYDAR:
Leaves (Dökülen, *Yeşil Alev*, 1991)
Water (Su, *Dünya bana aynısını anlatacak*, 1995)
Pitcher (Testi, *Dünya bana aynısını anlatacak*, 1995)
Virgin River (Erden Nehri, *Dünya bana aynısını anlatacak*, 1995; Ne Üzgün,
çiçek dünyaları, 1996; Süt Lotüsü, *Yeşil Alev*, 1991)
Seagulls (Martılar, *çiçek dünyaları*, 1996)
"In the insanity of turtles" (Aşk, *çiçek dünyalaıı*, 1996
A Sea Bird (Bir Deniz Kuşu, *çiçek dünyaları*, 1996)
Jacket (Ceket, *çiçek dünyaları*, 1996)
Gigi (Gigi, *Yeşil Alev*, 1991)
Baptismal Font (Vaftız Tepsisi, *Dünya bana aynısını anlatacak*, 1995)
His Winter Friend (Kış Arkadaşı, *Dünya bana aynısını anlatacak*, 1995)
Guillevic and the Leopard's Bed (Guilleviç Ve Leopar Yatağı, *Dünya banaı
aynısını anlatacak*, 1995)
Here It's Coming (İşte Gelmekte, *Yeşil Alev*, 1991)
"In my bed a wave covers me" (Su, *Yeşil Alev*, 1991)
No One Home (Biri, *Yeşil Alev*, 1991)

küçük İSKENDER:
souljam (*cangüncem*, 1996)
A Moment Please (lütfen, bir dakika, *cangüncem*, 1996)

DİDEM MADAK:
Sir, I want to Write Poems with Flowers (Çiçekli Şiirler Yazmak İstiyorum Bayım!,
Grapon Kağitları, 2000)

ZEYNEP SAYIN:
Pornography of the Image (*İmgenin Pornografisi*, 2003)

Designed by Samuel Retsov

∾

Text: 11 pt. Roman

∾

acid-free paper

∾

Printed by McNaughton & Gunn